CATHEDRAL CITY

A Look at Victorian Lichfield

by

HOWARD CLAYTON

Published by the Author at
" Rocklands "
Wissage Road
Lichfield

(1977)

Printed in Great Britain by
The Benhill Press Ltd., Brook Square, Rugeley, Staffs.

CONTENTS

ACKNOWLEDGMENTS

THE material for this book has been collected over a number of years, and from many different sources. I would like to thank the following institutions and persons for their help in my researches.

Lichfield Charter Trustees, for access to the City Muniments; Lichfield Public Library (Local History Collection); The William Salt Library, Stafford; Staffordshire County Record Office; The Staffordshire Regiment Museum, Lichfield; Birmingham Reference Library; The British Newspaper Library; The National Railway Museum, York; Lichfield Joint Record Office; The Library of the Institute of Bankers; The Library of the Institution of Civil Engineers; The South Staffordshire Waterworks Company; The Governor of H.M. Prison, Swinfen Hall; Prebendary E. C. Hill, Hon. Librarian, Lichfield Cathedral; Rev. Hesketh, Vicar of Weeford; Rev. Andrew Payne, Vicar of St. Michael's, Lichfield; Mr Dennis Birch, Lichfield; Mrs Madge Ebdon, Lichfield; and my son John Clayton who designed the dust jacket.

The following works have been consulted in preparing this book:
1. *A Sentimental Journey in and around Lichfield.* (Alfred Parker), Lomax, Lichfield, 1925.
2. *History of the Conduit Lands Trust.* (Percy Laithwaite), Lomax, Lichfield, 1945.
3. *Memorials of Sir Francis Chantry* 1839-72, (Holland) 1857.
4. *The Choral Revival in the Anglican Church,* 1839-72. (Bernarr Rainbow), Barrie and Jenkins, 1970.
5. *Argument in the Court of Common Pleas in Swinfen v Swinfen,* (Charles Rann Kennedy, Q.C.), 1857.
6. *Times Law Reports.*
7. *Minute Book,* Lichfield Board of Guardians.

And also the following periodicals:
The Illustrated London News.
Pictorial Times.
Staffordshire Advertiser.
Staffordshire Examiner.
Lichfield Mercury.
Birmingham Post.
Warwick and Warwickshire Advertiser.
Railway Magazine.

Foreword

The ancient City of Lichfield known as " Mother of the Midlands "—from a description by its most famous lexicographer Dr Samuel Johnson—owes much of its interesting history from its central position in the heart of England. Located at the intersection of two Roman roads, it has perpetuated into the modern era its convenience for communication and extended it to all forms of travel to all parts of the country. Between the ancient and modern, this Cathedral City experienced a time when the " world " passed it by. This book of Howard Clayton's covers that void and fulfils a literary need in respect of that period.

Written with humour, an intimate knowledge and an obviously great affection for the City, he has produced this imaginative record of that critical time in its history—a worthy successor to his "Coaching City"—introducing the humour, intrigue and tribulations in the lives of notable families at that time.

As Mayor at this time, I am proud to add this foreword and extend my congratulations to the author, acknowledging as I do, the tremendous research he has obviously undertaken to produce it.

MAYOR'S PARLOUR,
GUILDHALL,   ROBERT BLEWITT,
LICHFIELD.   *The Right Worshipful,*
MARCH 1977.   *the Mayor of Lichfield.*

CHAPTER 1

Lichfield in 1832

IN October 1832 the Princess Victoria, then a girl of twelve, paid a visit to Lichfield with her mother, the Duchess of Kent.

The visit was part of a programme of tours to various parts of the United Kingdom arranged by Sir John Conroy the Comptroller of the Duchess of Kent's Household. Ostensibly the purpose was to introduce to the British people the person who might be their future Queen, but as far as Sir John was concerned it was much more a case of promoting the interests of the Duchess of Kent. In the event of Victoria succeeding to the throne before the age of eighteen (which at that time seemed more than likely), there would be a good chance of her mother becoming Regent, which in turn would advance the position of Sir John Conroy. Sir John and the Duchess worked together to this end, but as it happened King William IV thwarted their plans by living until his niece was a month over eighteen.

The trip to Lichfield was made while Victoria and her mother were staying at Shugborough as the guests of Lord Lichfield, and its object was to visit the cathedral. As their carriage turned from Beacon Street into the Cathedral Close, the sight that met their eyes must have been a curious one, quite unlike that which one can see today.

The cathedral had been restored by Bishop Hacket after the destruction of the Civil War, but throughout the 18th century little work was done on it. It was a period during which the Church of England was largely moribund; a period of sinecures and pluralism, of port wine and periwigs. Most churches suffered from neglect and Lichfield Cathedral was no exception.

By the end of the 18th century neglect had reached the point where something had to be done if the building were to remain standing. In 1788 the Dean and Chapter called in the celebrated architect James Wyatt to carry out a restoration.

Wyatt was a local man, born in 1746 at Blackbrook Farm, Weeford, a few miles south of Lichfield. His father, Benjamin Wyatt, was the architect of Swinfen Hall, between Weeford and Lichfield (now part of one of Her Majesty's Prisons). As a youth, James Wyatt's talents came to the notice of Sir Walter Bagot of Blithfield, who took him to Italy when he was sixteen. Sir Walter was British Ambassador in Rome, and he arranged for Wyatt to study architecture for two years in Venice and four years in Rome. At the end of this time he came back to England and set up in practice in London.

The field in which he worked was that of the wealthy land-owner's country house, his interior work at Heveningham Hall, Suffolk, being one of his best-known works. His output was great, but nevertheless his critics accused him of indolence. William Beckford for whom Wyatt worked at Fonthill Abbey, in Wiltshire, is reputed to have said, " If Wyatt can get near a big fire and have a bottle by him, he cares for nothing else."

Fonthill, the work for which Wyatt is principally remembered, was totally different from his other works, being a Gothic fantasy designed for an eccentric and fabulously wealthy client. It had a central tower 225 feet high (which collapsed twice) and a thousand men worked on it day and night for eleven years. The collapse of the tower cannot be blamed on Wyatt; the contractor confessed on his death bed that he had omitted proper foundations!

Fonthill was begun in 1797 when Wyatt was engaged on the restoration of Lichfield Cathedral; perhaps it was from here that he received the Gothic inspiration.

Much of his work at Lichfield consisted of necessary structural restoration. The walls of the nave were being forced outwards, and to lighten the load on them Wyatt removed the stone vaulting on five of the bays and replaced it with lath and plaster. For the same reason he added two large buttresses to the south transept.

In addition to this work the centre spire was rebuilt, the building re-roofed and the interior remodelled in accordance with the wishes of the Dean and Chapter, a process which involved the lavish use of Roman cement (stucco). So enthusiastic did they become over the use of this material that after the death of James Wyatt in 1813 they extended it to the outside of the building. Between 1820 and 1822, under the guiding hand of Joseph Potter, a Lichfield architect, they covered the whole of the west front with Roman cement completely obliterating the decoration and mouldings.

The west front is one of the glories of Lichfield Cathedral. It consists of a richly decorated screen flanked on either side by towers surmounted by octagonal spires. As completed in the 13th century the decoration consisted of 113 statues of " Kings, Patriarchs, Prophets, Fathers and Apostles." These were set in arcading with an intricate decoration of trefoils, quatrefoils and cinqfoils, the figures themselves being gilded.

The statues were damaged during the Civil War when the Cathedral was besieged, and finally demolished at the end of the 18th century by a Dean who fancied that some of the figures nodded to him as he went into the building at service time.

By 1820 the stonework of the west front was in such a poor state that Dean Woodhouse adopted the drastic measure just mentioned of encasing the whole in Roman cement. Not content with this, he sent Mr Potter's son to Wells to make drawings of the figures on the west front there, and these were then cast in Roman cement and applied to the lower stage of the west front of Lichfield Cathedral.

This, then, was the grotesque sight that met the eyes of the young Princess Victoria and her mother as they turned into the Close on that October afternoon in 1832. Waiting at the west door to greet his royal visitors was the perpetrator of these horrors, John Chappel Woodhouse, Dean of Lichfield, and by his side the Senior Bailiff (Mayor) of the City of Lichfield, Alderman Thomas George

Lomax. Mr Lomax was the owner of a bookselling and publishing business at the corner of Bird Street and Market Street; as " Lomax's Successors " it is still remembered by many people in Lichfield.

They escorted their guests inside the cathedral. The long nave was bare, used only by curious visitors who wandered around looking at the few memorials that remained. So, too, were the transepts, except that in the south transept the Dean occasionally held his Consistory Court. Only the choir and the Lady Chapel were used for worship. These had been joined together by Mr Wyatt at the request of the Dean and Chapter thus encapsulating the choir and congregation in one long room, sealed off as effectively as possible from the rest of the cathedral. At the west end of the choir he had built a screen from parts of the mediaeval reredos which he had discovered. Those parts which were missing he made good with Roman cement. Above this screen was the organ, and above that the space up to the roof was filled in with glass. Entrance to the choir was through baize-covered doors in the screen.

On either side of the choir the arches were filled in with masonry, rendered, of course, with Roman cement and this was carried right up to the Lady Chapel. The altar was placed at the east end of the Lady Chapel. The purpose of all this was to make the place warmer in winter for those worshipping in it, a purpose which, according to contemporary accounts, was not achieved. The Prebendaries and Canons had their stalls at the west end of the choir, under canopies made of the ubiquitous Roman cement; the congregation sat in high box pews lined in baize which extended into the Lady Chapel.

As Dean Woodhouse took his royal visitors around this interior he was no doubt at pains to show them the memorial to his two little granddaughters. This, the work of Sir Francis Chantrey, R.A., had been placed in the cathedral five years before and had become one of the main points of interest for visitors. It still is today.

The story behind Chantrey's "Sleeping Children" is tragic enough, even for an age when infant mortality was high and few families grew up without some deaths among the children. It begins in April 1801 when Dean Woodhouse's daughter, Ellen Jane, married a young clergyman, William Robinson. Preferment came swiftly and before long he was Rector of Stoke-on-Trent, and a few years later a Prebendary of Lichfield Cathedral. His career was cut short, however, by illness and he died of consumption in March 1812, while still in his thirties, leaving his wife with two little girls.

The following year, while mother and daughters were staying at Bath, the elder of the two girls (also named Ellen Jane) was preparing for bed when she went to reach for something on the mantelpiece. There was a fire in the hearth; her nightdress caught alight and she died from the burns received.

Before another year had passed the stricken mother received yet another blow when her younger child, Marianne, sickened and died while they were in London. In three years the whole of Mrs Robinson's family had been lost to her. In her distress she turned to Mr Nicholson, the drawing master who had taught her and the two girls, and asked him for his help in securing some likeness of the dead child. He suggested Chantrey, and went to see him the same day. The sculptor returned to Mrs Robinson's house with him and made a cast of the dead child's face, and in a long interview with the mother learnt that she wished him to make a memorial to her two children to be placed in Lichfield Cathedral.

Mrs Robinson had a very clear idea of what she wanted. Before Chantrey had left her she had explained to him her feelings when, in the past, before retiring to bed, she had watched them asleep in each other's arms. That was how she wanted them represented. She also requested Chantrey to pay a visit to Ashbourne church in Derbyshire, to see a memorial there, the style of which he was to copy.

So it was that a few days later he went to Ashbourne to view the monument to Penelope Boothby, daughter of Sir Brooke Boothby a gentleman well-known in Lichfield society as a dilettante and as an associate of the late Dr Erasmus Darwin, but more especially as the man who had recently procured for Lichfield Cathedral the magnificent stained glass from Herckenrode which now adorned the Lady Chapel*.

Penelope Boothby was an only child, and when she died at the age of five in 1791 the loss of " this frail barque " meant the end of her parents' marriage. Her father engaged Thomas Banks to make the memorial, a figure of the little girl asleep, sculpted in Cararra marble. It marked a complete break from the stylistic Baroque of 18th century funeral monuments; instead the child is portrayed in her normal clothes and as natural as possible in appearance.

Furnished with these directions, Chantrey returned to his home and made a small model of the proposed memorial, almost exactly as it was afterwards executed. Mrs Robinson approved, and work began on a life-size marble group of the two little girls—the " Sleeping Children " as it was to become known.

The carving of the monument was entrusted to one of Chantrey's assistants, Mr F. A. Legé, and as the work proceeded he suggested an alteration to Chantrey—the addition of a bunch of snowdrops in the hand of the younger sister. The designer agreed, and so this little symbolic touch was added to the memorial.

The work was completed in time to be shown at the Royal Academy Exhibition of 1816, and here it was a sensation. According to a contemporary account, " Such was the press to see these children in the London Exhibition, that there was no getting near them: mothers, with tears in their eyes, lingered and went away, and returned; while Canova's figures of Hebe and Terpsichore stood almost unheeded by their side."

---

* The Herckenrode glass dates from 1530 to 1540. It came from the dissolved Abbey of Herckenrode, near Liège, and was purchased by Sir Brooke in 1802 for the sum of £200. He brought it to England and sold it to the Dean and Chapter of Lichfield for the same amount. It was fitted to the windows of the Lady Chapel in 1811.

The " Sleeping Children " was placed in Lichfield Cathedral in 1817 and has been a source of interest to visitors ever since. It anticipated by some years the Victorian taste for the sentimental, but probably most of the interest is due to the fact that the memorial is such a contrast to the others in the cathedral, which are all, without exception, those of Bishops and Deans. Added to this is the element of curiosity, for nowhere is the story of the " Sleeping Children " explained.

Mrs Robinson's tragic story did not end with the deaths of her first family. In 1817 she married again, this time to Hugh Dyke Acland of Killerton, in Devon, and in this connection it is interesting to note that in later years Chantrey was commissioned to produce another " Sleeping Child," this time the daughter of Sir Thomas Dyke Acland of Killerton.

After a few years the unfortunate lady lost her second husband, again through illness, leaving her this time with an only son, Hugh Woodhouse Acland, born in 1818. In 1835 she was married, for the third time, to Richard Hinckley, a Lichfield attorney, and they made their home at Beacon Place.

Beacon Place and the surrounding park had been inherited by Mrs Robinson from her father in 1833. Dean Woodhouse had purchased it from the Hand family. It was a country estate in the midst of a town. About an hundred acres in extent, the park was reputedly laid out by Lancelot " Capability " Brown, at the same time that the house was built.* Beacon Place was approached by three drives; the main entrance from Beacon Street opposite what is now Anson Avenue, another from the old Walsall Road (now Christ Church Lane) and the third from the Home Farm, in Lower Sandford Street.

In 1847, as a memorial to all those she had lost, Mrs Hinckley built a new church at Leomansley, on the west side of Lichfield. It stood just inside Beacon Park, by the western entrance and

---

* As Beacon Place does not appear on John Snape's map of Lichfield published in 1781, and as " Capability " Brown died in 1783, this is unlikely.

within view of her home. To go with it she provided a vicarage and a school, and endowed the living. So there came into being Christ Church, the newest of Lichfield's parish churches. But tragedy still dogged the life of its foundress, for one of the first burials in its churchyard was that of her only son. In 1865 her third husband was laid to rest beside him, but Ellen Jane Hinckley lived on to reach the ripe old age of 87, the survivor of all her three families.

*   *   *

Princess Victoria and her mother returned to Shugborough after their visit to the cathedral. On the way, so tradition has it, she felt thirsty, and they stopped at a farmhouse just outside Lichfield on the Stafford Road. Today the house is a farmhouse no longer, and stands well within the boundaries of the city, but in the room where she was received her signed portrait still hangs on the wall. She gave it as a gift, years later when she was Queen, to the late owner's great-grandfather.*

Shugborough was one of a number of country houses around Lichfield which formed a background for the social life of the wealthier landlords of the district. A fascinating account of this society has been left in her diary† by Miss Bagot, a niece of Lord Bagot of Blithfield, who lived in the Close at Lichfield in the house next to the Deanery. Among the many human touches which emerge from this narrative are those connected with Miss Bagot's love of gardening and the differences of opinion with her neighbour, Dean Woodhouse, which arose from this. She rented a piece of garden at the back of the Deanery, but the Dean would not allow her access through his own garden and in consequence she was forced to walk round into Beacon Street and Gaia Lane to reach her plot. Referring to this on one occasion, she wonders ruefully how many miles she has to walk in a year because of this detour. There was also the episode when she wished to build a greenhouse in her garden but the Dean objected. She did, however, manage to build an ornamental pool and brought back gold-fish for it from Birmingham "in a bladder"—a remarkably modern touch for 1820!

---

* The author is indebted to the late Major E. B. Burke for this information.
† William Salt Library, Stafford.

Miss Bagot's diary starts in 1819, when she was 45 years old, and continues until 1843—three years before her death. It begins with a reference to Lord Anglesey, one of the heroes of Waterloo, and near the end mentions an experience totally different from anything she had encountered before.

" December 1837. I went one day to see the rail road trains come in. It is quite overcoming and made me ready to cry, as if I had seen a ship launched . . ."

Throughout the diary there are references to parties at country houses in the neighbourhood—Shugborough, Blithfield, Shenstone Park, Drakelow and many others. Here is an account of dinner at Meaford Hall, Stone, the home of Admiral Lord St Vincent, victor of the famous battle against the Spaniards on St Valentine's Day, 1797, from which he took his title.

" 4th November, 1822. We all went to dine at Lord St Vincent's, who received me cordially—Martial Law is established in his house, as everybody does as he bids them—he told Lord Northesk and Lord Rosehill to hand Lady Neve and myself to dinner before greater folk than ourselves, but we could only do as we were bid— we were a party of seventeen, all our names pin'd upon the chairs at which we were to sit at dinner. Lord Vincent himself eighty-eight with all his faculties as shrewd as ever—he wears a blue coat buttoned to the chin and a splendid star—a blue velvet cap without any hair to be seen—the costume however singularly suits him."

Fourteen years later Miss Bagot was still able to enjoy a good party.

" 15th September, 1836. Took Mr Mucklestone in my fly and went about six o'clock to Manley Hall for the opening of that beautiful place—we were about 100. I did not get home till six, and left them waltzing as if they had just begun, to a fresh set of candles."

Manley Hall, near Weeford, was built by Admiral Manley whose brother had served in the French wars as an officer in the Austrian army and later as Adjutant General of the Papal Guard. It had a short life as country houses go. After some years as a boys' school it was demolished in the 1960s.

Mr Mucklestone, Miss Bagot's escort on this occasion, was the Subchanter—one of the Priest Vicars of Lichfield Cathedral. A widower, he maintained his cosy bachelor establishment in a pleasant little Georgian house which is now Number 56, Beacon Street.

Of all Miss Bagot's social engagements, though, the most interesting are those connected with archery. There had been a vogue for this sport in Staffordshire since 1799, when a society known as The Bowmen of Staffordshire had been formed under the patronage of the Earl of Harrowby. It languished during the Napoleonic Wars, as many of the members were army officers, but was revived in the 1820s. At the same time a similar society was formed by Lord Bagot from among his relations and friends. Here is how Miss Bagot describes their first meeting.
" July 31st, 1822. Louisa took me to Stafford to buy a pelisse for Lord Bagot's Archery."
" August 9th, 1822. Went with the Levetts to the Blithfield Archery. I have seldom enjoyed a diversion so much. We were somewhere about 130 people on the ground, the place looking quite beautiful. Levett won a gold and topaz seal. We were about 38 relations in some degree or other—Lord Bagot appeared to great advantage. The dinner was spread in the two drawing rooms and the conservatory and the little library. A shower of rain after dinner prevented much shooting—there were several tents so that people were not much inconvenienced—a few quadrilles were danced. I introduced partners to Charlotte and Caroline and returned to Shugborough."

Present on this occasion was another diarist, General William Dyott of Freeford, and he too has left us a record of the day.
" August 9th, 1822. I had the honour to attend a great party at Blithfield given by Lord Bagot; the first meeting of a new society called the Needwood Foresters, consisting of a number of neighbouring families, for the display of skill in archery. The company assembled at 12 o'clock. Butts had been made and tents pitched on the pleasure ground adjoining the house. About 130 assembled and the ladies and gentlemen members of the society amused themselves shooting until 3 o'clock, attended by the band of the

Staffs. Militia, when the musick struck up " The Roast Beef of Old England " and the company sat down in the house to venison and turtle in abundance. Tea and coffee was prepared and the young ones turned to and amused themselves with quadrilles.

It was intended to resume shooting after dinner, but unfortunately it rained."

Under the leadership of Lord Bagot the Needwood Foresters became established as a permanent society. They met four times a year, at Blithfield, Byrkley Lodge (the home of Edward Sneyd), Hollybush Hall (Thomas Kirkpatrick Hall), and Dunstall Lodge (Charles Arkwright). These meetings, we are told, " were conducted with a degree of Baronial Splendour unequalled in the United Kingdom."

At Blithfield Lord Bagot demolished the Rectory and built a new one elsewhere in order to lay out the Archery Ground. A wide lawn some 150 yards in length, surrounded by woods and bordered on one side by a Gothic ruin, the remains of the old Rectory, it has still today the romantic atmosphere which was so much sought after in the early years of the 19th century, an atmosphere engendered by the novels of Sir Walter Scott.

As with all archery societies at this period, the Needwood Foresters had their own uniform, obligitory at the butts and when dining together. A splendid example of the men's dress exists at Blithfield Hall today, in the collection of Nancy, Lady Bagot. This is Lord Bagot's own uniform, and consists of a frock coat in green melton cloth with a rolled collar. It is single-breasted, cut straight in front at the bottom to come just below the knees and fitted with gilt buttons engraved " The Needwood Foresters." This was worn with white trousers, a white waistcoat and a peaked cap of the same cloth as the coat.

The ladies wore a green pelisse and a straw hat with two green feathers—the latter item, according to Mrs Charles Bagot, costing five guineas, although of the coarsest straw.

The meetings of the Needwood Foresters continued for the next five years and the last meeting was held in September 1827. It was as magnificent as usual, and as well attended. But for some unknown reason it was never repeated. The fashion for archery languished for the next twenty years, to be revived in the middle of the century. Lichfield had its Society of Archers, founded in 1851 by Mr Manley of Manley Hall. Richard Greene of Stowe House donated their trophies; a silver bugle and baldrick for the gentlemen and a silver quiver for the ladies. The Society lasted until the second World War; then, like so many other institutions it faded away. Where, one wonders, are the trophies today?*

One sport which did not fade away however, was the game of cricket which has flourished in Lichfield for the last 150 years. Just when the city first had a cricket club is not clear, but the *Lichfield Mercury* for the 14th July, 1830 carries an account of a match between the Lichfield Club and the Tamworth Club. The scores were low by modern standards, but a good time seems to have been had by all. It is interesting to recall that only twenty years before the principal amusement would have been bull and bear baiting, prize-fighting and cock-fighting, with heavy wagering on the results. (Even in the cricket match, it should be noted, " Odds were offered and taken on both sides.") The country was moving away from the rather brutish habits of Regency England which made such a contrast with the elegance of the period in other respects and through the reign of Victoria this change was to continue.

The *Lichfield Mercury* had no sports page as yet, but it devoted half a column to the report of the match, as follows.

---

* As this book was going to press, the trophies came to light, having languished for many years in the vaults of a Lichfield bank. They are now in the possession of the present Lichfield Society of Archers.

CRICKET MATCH

BETWEEN THE LICHFIELD AND TAMWORTH CLUBS

This match, which excited great interest in the neighbourhood, came off at Lichfield on Monday last. It was played in the spacious field called Levett's Field, which was generously offered by Mr Webb * for that purpose. A marquee was set up which contained refreshments for the combatants. The Lichfield Club was the favourite, as they had won the previous match which was played at Tamworth a fortnight ago. Odds, however, were offered and taken on both sides. A numerous concourse of people were assembled, and seats were provided for the ladies. The operations commenced at about half-past eleven o'clock, and concluded a short time before five o'clock. The Lichfield Club were declared victorious. The numbers were as follows: —

LICHFIELD		TAMWORTH	
FIRST INNINGS		FIRST INNINGS	
T. Webb, bld by Thacker	1	G. Thacker, bld by Baggaley	0
A. Hitchcock, not out	29	G. Bourne, bld by Webb	8
Chawner, bld by Thacker	0	Spencer, bld by Baggaley	0
W. Parr, run out	1	T. Parr, ditto	0
T. Hitchcock, bld by Thacker	0	Jervis, bld by Webb	9
Griffith, ditto	0	Woodhouse, run out	0
Baggaley, bld by Bourne	0	Capenhurst, bld by Hitchcock	3
Ward, bld by Thacker	9	R. Brown, caught by Hitchcock	10
Yeld, ditto	0	T. Freer, bld by Webb	0
Osborne, run out	0	J. Stretton, leg before wicket	9
J. Wildrey, bld by Woodhouse	2	Harrison, not out	0
	42		39
Byes	3	Byes	4
Wide Balls	2	Wide Balls	1
No Balls	1		
	48		44

---

* Mr. Webb, landlord of the George Hotel, had a large posting stables close to Levett's Field.

SECOND INNINGS		SECOND INNINGS	
T. Webb, not out	23	G. Thacker, bld by Webb	0
A. Hitchcock, run out	3	G. Bourne, ditto	19
Chawner, leg before wicket	3	Spencer, bld Baggaley	0
W. Parr, bld Whitehouse	1	T. Parr, caught by Osborne	0
T. Hitchcock, ditto	0	Jervis, bld by Webb	10
Griffith, bld by Thacker	0	Woodhouse, ditto	4
Baggaley, ditto	0	Capenhurst, bld Baggaley	1
Ward, bld Woodhouse	1	R. Brown, ditto	1
Yeld, bld by Thacker	7	T. Freer, not out	0
Osborne, bld by Woodhouse	2	J. Stretton, bld Baggaley	2
J. Wildrey, ditto	3	Harrison, ditto	1
	43		38
Byes	4	Byes	3
No Balls	2		
	49		41

Lichfield—total of both innings 97

Tamworth—total of both innings 82

At half-past six the members of both clubs sat down to a sumptuous dinner, provided by Mr Sharp, at the George Hotel. A number of other gentlemen, patrons of this truly manly game, joined them. About fifty gentlemen sat down. Mr Chawner of the Lichfield Club presided, and Mr William Parr, the Secretary, acted as croupier*. After the usual loyal toasts were given, the chairman proposed the Members of the Tamworth Club, and paid them a well merited compliment for their gentlemanly and friendly demeanour during the arduous struggle and for the good temper and kindly feeling they had displayed in their defeat. Mr Brown returned thanks and proposed the Lichfield Club; this toast was suitably acknowledged by the Chairman. The healths of the ladies, the umpires and various other toasts were given. Mr Harrison, of the Tamworth Club, and several other gentlemen, contributed greatly to the harmony of the evening by their excellent songs, and the parties did not separate until a late hour. We hear another match is on the *tapis* but the preliminaries are not finally arranged."

---

* Croupier; Defined by the Oxford Dictionary as, "raker-in of money at gaming table; vice-chairman at dinners etc." Presumably the latter meaning is intended in this case.

The Lichfield in which the above events took place was a
pleasant place to live in. At the 1831 census its population had
been 6,499, living in 1,034 houses—an average of just over six
people to a house which in the context of the conditions of that
period could certainly not be considered overcrowding, especially
when one considers that the houses of the wealthier families had
at least one servant living in them for every member of the family.
Unlike other midland towns, Lichfield did not experience periodic
outbreaks of cholera and other epidemics caused by the close
proximity of cesspools and wells supplying domestic water. For
centuries the Conduit Lands Trust had supplied pure water to all
the inhabitants, piped from their springs at Aldershaw. The
Improvement Commissioners had installed an underground sewer-
age system, had paved the streets and made provision for cleaning
them and had lighted the city with gas. On the whole it was a law
abiding place—the City Gaol and House of Correction in the
basement of the Guildhall had eleven rooms and cells, but at the
enquiry held by the Commissioners in 1833 it was stated that these
were often empty for months on end.

Education was provided for boys by the Free Grammar School,
a foundation of Edward VI, at which there were six free scholars
(others paid one and a half guineas in the Upper School and one
guinea in the Lower School). Minor's English School in Bore
Street took thirty free scholars and there was also a National
School for boys and girls in Frog Lane. At the Girls' School of
Industry in Dam Street there were 64 poor pupils, while various
private Academies and Seminaries in different parts of the city
catered for the better-off. The Headmaster of the National School,
Mr Allen, was also Manager of the Savings Bank, founded in 1816.
In November 1832 its deposits amounted to £27,576 8s. 9d. This
represented the savings of 790 individuals and societies.

In Tamworth Street a Mendicity Office dealt with the problem
of vagrants, while nearby a Free Dispensary provided some relief
for the sick who could not afford the fees of an apothecary or
surgeon. For the destitute there were workhouses maintained by
the three parishes—St Mary's in Sandford Street, St Chad's in

Stowe Street and St Michael's on Greenhill. The accommodation was basic, the conditions often slovenly, but there was not yet the harsh discipline that was to come with the setting up of the unions.

The tradesmen of the city were still organised in seven Free Companies—Tailors, Bakers, Butchers, Saddlers, Smiths, Cordwainers and Weavers. These descendants of the mediaeval guilds had already lost most of their original functions as the Industrial Revolution and the factory system rendered them obsolete but they survived because membership of them conferred an important privilege. Freemen of a company, duly enrolled and sworn by the Town Clerk and paying Scot and Lot (city rates), could vote at Parliamentary Elections. This was valuable at a time when the suffrage was limited and votes were unashamedly bought by both political parties. As the vote was extended to more and more people, and with the reform of the franchise, the last reason for the retention of the companies disappeared and so did the companies themselves, with one exception. The Company of Smiths, or to give it its full title, the Worshipful Company of Smiths, Goldsmiths, Cardmakers and Ironmongers, Pewterers and Braziers, Plumbers, Cutlers, Nailors and Spurriers survived and exists to this day, holding its Mayoral Court and Annual Feast in Guildhall at the beginning of each year. Little trace remains of the others, though the minute book of the Cordwainers Company still exists in a Manchester library, preserved by an antiquary of that city. While passing through Lichfield towards the end of the last century he was approached in one of the city hostelries by the last survivor of the Lichfield Cordwainers who, being short of cash and in need of a drink, sold him the book for five shillings. Sic transit gloria!

Among the inhabitants of the city at this time were to be found, in addition to the ecclesiastic establishment, 2 architects, 10 lawyers, 4 proctors and notaries public, 2 bankers, 3 medical practitioners, 3 booksellers, a carpet manufacturer and a rope maker. To cater for the refreshment and sustenance of the 6,499 citizens there were 55 inns and 17 beer-houses. For sustenance of a more intellectual kind there were two circulating libraries and a subscription library, while those with a musical bent could join the

St Cecilia Society. For many years this body had enriched the social life of the city with its concerts, for which the gentlemen met at the Swan Inn and after dining there made their way up to Vicars' Hall in the Close, where the ladies joined them for the music. Lichfield also had its own theatre in Bore Street.

While being a pleasant place for those who lived in it, Lichfield was much favoured by the surrounding gentry as a meeting place for county balls, race meetings and similar functions. It was still very much a Jane Austin type of society, very provincial in character, in spite of the efforts of a group of the city's inhabitants during the previous decade to turn it into a fashionable spa.

For this was the golden age of English spas. Beau Brummel at Bath and the Duke of Devonshire at Buxton had shown the way, and at Leamington Dr Jephson had made a fortune from the waters. Not only was he earning as much as £20,000 a year from his gout-ridden patients, but at the same time, as Leamington grew from a small Warwickshire village to a fashionable spa, Jephson's business acumen was applied to considerable advantage in the field of property speculation. Many others attempted to follow his example in the midlands; Ashby-de-la-Zouch had some success although the water had to be brought from coal pits at Moira in large tanks on canal boats, but others such as Willoughby Spa near Dunchurch and Victoria Spa near Stratford-on-Avon failed to excite any interest at all. Lichfield seems to have been another of these also-rans.

On the face of it, there must have seemed a good potential for turning the city into a second Leamington. It was an easy place to get to, it had all the amenities just mentioned and it had a mineral spring near St Chad's Church, the waters of which, according to a local chemist, " were similar to those of Tunbridge Wells." Such must have been the thoughts in the minds of a group of Lichfield citizens who met together in the autumn of 1824 and issued the following statement.*

---

* Statement and Minute book, Lichfield City Muniments.

" We who are named herein being desirous of establishing hot and cold baths in the City of Lichfield do agree to become subscribers thereto and to attend a meeting to be holden in the Town Hall on Friday 24th inst. at twelve o'clock (at noon) to consider the best means of carrying this into execution. The subscription for one share not to exceed £10.

T. Ferris, John Dyott, John Power, Stephen Simpson, George Hodgson, Thomas Green, S. Mellor, William Gill, James Palmer, Ley Brookes, C. Bingham, Thomas Rowley, Charles Chawner, E. S. Remington, Thomas White."

The meeting was duly held and the proceedings recorded in the Minute Book as follows.

" At a meeting held on 24th September, 1824, pursuant to the foregoing resolution.
Present Thomas Jarvis Esq., Mr Dyott, Rev. E. Remington, Mr Mellor, Mr Rowley, Mr S. Simpson, Mr Dodson, Mr White.
Resolved That hot and cold and vapour baths shall be established in the City of Lichfield.

That if sufficient funds shall be raised a reading room and the Permanent Library shall, with the consent of the subscribers, be proposed to be attached thereto.

That every subscriber of £10 shall be entitled annually to twelve transferable tickets for bathing—and of £20 to £25 to twenty such tickets for bathing in the salt or fresh baths.

That subscribers shall pay two shillings each time of bathing in a hot bath, and one-and-sixpence in a cold bath, whether salt or fresh water.

That when sums amounting to £500 shall have been subscribed the subscribers shall be called together to consider the best situation and plan for the proposed baths.

That the subscriptions shall be paid into the hands of Messers Scott & Co. Bankers, when called for."

Mr Stephen Simpson, at that time Town Clerk of Lichfield, appears to have been one of the chief promoters of this enterprise, and the minute book contains a letter to him from a Mr Dalhouse of Leamington, from whom he had obviously been seeking enlightenment on the subject of baths. Not a very helpful epistle, it ran as follows:

Leamington,

30th October, 1824.

" Dear Sir,

On my return from Liverpool I found your letter and can only say that the best Bath I have seen for warm bathing is one at Bedworth depository.

My brother the Colonel says that the best he knows are at Brighton, but I would not have you go to much expense for I have known people lose both their strength and appetite by bathing in both simple or medicated water. There is in the Bible what is not to be found in Christian knowledge, and there is in saline springs what no man can give. Medical men prate about warm bathing, and I have no objection to such learned prate, because it gives them a disposition to seek for health and strength where it can be found. Application to business and economy of money, and warm bathing from home is what wisdom would recommend, if you can find such at Lichfield.

With respect to the cost of baths I know nothing."

Whether it was due to the effect of Mr Dalhouse's letter or to the difficulty of raising the £500 will probably never be known, but that is the last we hear of the idea of Lichfield Spa.

CHAPTER II

The Last of the Coaches

1837, the year of Queen Victoria's accession to the throne, was a bad one for Lichfield.

For the past fifty years the city had enjoyed a period of prosperity during which its position at the crossroads of two trunk routes—one between London and Liverpool, and the other between Birmingham and Sheffield—had made it a centre of the coaching trade. Easy communication brought both commerce and society to Lichfield, as well as those trades which supplied the coaches, such as corn merchants, horse keepers, harness-makers, etc. The city's coaching inns flourished, and the centre of the town was rebuilt in the red Georgian brick we see today.

By 1837, however, it was obviously that the coaches had had their day. Seven years before, George Stephenson had completed the Liverpool and Manchester Railway, which was an immediate commercial success, and now it was being joined to Birmingham by the Grand Junction Railway. At the same time George Stephenson's son Robert was hard at work on the London and Birmingham, and another line was being built between Birmingham and Derby. By 1838 all these three railways had been completed, and Lichfield's coaches had disappeared, for they were quite unable to compete with the new form of transport. The last mail coach through Lichfield ran on 11th April, 1838, and after that the city rapidly became a backwater in which the only thing that flourished was the bankruptcy court. It was to remain like this for the next ten years.

The position was summed up very well by Alderman Lomax in evidence which he gave to a Parliamentary committee a few years later and which ran as follows—

" Thomas George Lomax of the City of Lichfield, Bookseller and Town Councillor has been Mayor of Lichfield and resided there upwards of thirty-five years.

" The want of railway accommodation is severely felt in Lichfield. Till the London and Birmingham, Grand Junction, and Derby Railways were made, the travelling through Lichfield was very great. The London and Liverpool, London and Chester, Bristol, Birmingham and Sheffield, and Wolverhampton, Walsall and Sheffield Mails and Coaches passed through Lichfield, which through traffic is now diverted by circuitous lines of railways.

" In the year 1835 the following coaches passed through Lichfield:

To London	5	a day.
„ Liverpool	4 „	„
„ Manchester	1 „	„
„ Birmingham	9 „	„
„ Sheffield	6 „	„
„ Walsall	4 „	„
„ Wolverhampton	2 „	„
Total	31	

" A parcel might then be sent almost any hour to Walsall, Birmingham or Sheffield; it can now only be sent at eight o'clock each morning, or by a single-horse mailcart to Tamworth at seven o'clock in the evening.

" Some idea of the present circuitous mode of transmission may be formed from the following statement.

" Walsall is nine miles from Lichfield. Parcels must either go to Tamworth (which place is seven and a half miles from Lichfield), thence by the Midland Railway to Birmingham (which is seventeen and a half miles), thence by the Grand Junction Railway to Walsall, (which is 10 miles), being thirty-four and a half miles with two stoppages and changes instead of nine and a half mile direct; or they must go to Birmingham (which is sixteen miles from Lichfield) and then by the Grand Junction Railway to Walsall (ten miles, making twenty-six miles). Or they may go to Stafford (which is seventeen miles from Lichfield) and then by the Grand Junction Railway to Walsall (which is twenty miles).

" The conveyance of a small parcel to Walsall used to be charged eightpence, which is now one shilling and sixpence and great uncertainty in punctual carriage."

The merchants and tradesmen of Lichfield saw their businesses declining as the city became a rural backwater, but were powerless to prevent it happening, though at least one attempt was made. The previous year, in December 1836, a group of prominent Lichfield citizens had met one evening in committee in the old Guildhall in Bore Street, to discuss the matter which was causing so much anxiety in the city.

In the chair was Mr Richard Green, banker, of Stowe House, and among those present were Thomas Rowley M.D., the Mayor of Lichfield; John Sultzer, a carpet manufacturer whose works were at Pones Mill; the Reverend William Gresley, curate of St Chad's Church, and Harvey Wyatt, land agent, of Barton-under-Needwood.

As they talked the quiet of the winter's evening was broken by the clatter of horses' hooves on cobbles and the strident notes of a coaching horn. It was the ' Standard ' stage coach drawing out from the inn yard of the ' Old Crown ' a few yards down the street, on the start of its journey to Derby. The significance of the sound was not lost on them; they were here to discuss the decline of the coaches, the advent of the railroad and the effect of these changes on the future development of Lichfield.

Already the lines from London to Birmingham and from Birmingham to Liverpool were in being and almost ready for use, and now news had been received of plans to build a railway from Stafford to Rugby, which would pass a mile to the east of Lichfield and would be known as the 'Manchester and South Union Railway.' The promoters, as the name implied, were Manchester businessmen who wanted a more direct route between their city and London, avoiding Birmingham. The news had resulted in a public meeting being called in Lichfield and the setting up of a 'Railway Committee' the aim of which was to ensure that Lichfield's interests were brought to the notice of the promoters of the 'Manchester and South Union.'

On the principle of " if you can't beat 'em, join 'em," the Lichfield Railway Committee, seeing that the city's coaching trade was doomed, hoped that something might be saved from the wreck by persuading the new railway company to bring their line through the town. They had little success however, for the most obvious route for a railway was along the low ground to the east of the city; to bring a line through the centre would have meant heavy engineering works to the north and south, where the land rises, and the promoters obviously did not consider that Lichfield was important enough to warrant the extra expense.

The next best thing was a branch line, terminating in the city, and it was with this in mind that the Railway Committee had met in the Guildhall on this December evening.

The result of the committee's deliberations became known a few days later when the following notice appeared in the ' Staffordshire Examiner,' a newspaper published in Lichfield.

SOUTH UNION RAILWAY

AT a MEETING of the COMMITTEE, appointed to communicate with the Committee of the Manchester South Union Railway Company, as to the best means of securing the interests of the City of Lichfield, in reference to the undertaking, held at the Guildhall, on Wednesday, the 14th December, 1836

RICHARD GREENE, Esquire, in the Chair,

It was Resolved, upon the motion of Harvey Wyatt, Esq., seconded by the Mayor, that a Branch Railroad, from the main line at Pones Mill, for the conveyance of goods, coals, &c., passing north of Stowe Pool, and terminating in Lombard-street, opposite the residence of Charles Simpson, Esq., or thereabouts, as may be eventually considered most desirable, and likewise the construction of a commodious common road, for the convenience of passengers to the main line, is best calculated to promote the interests and convenience of the City of Lichfield; and the Committee of the Manchester South Union Railway Company are requested to take such

steps to secure the accommodation as may appear necessary, the consent
of the proprietors through whose property it is proposed to bring the Branch
Railway and Road having been obtained.

It was further Resolved, on the motion of John Sultzer, Esquire,
seconded by the Rev. William Gresley, that this Committee having examined
the plans of Railways deposited by the Stafford and Rugeley Company, and
also the plans deposited by the Manchester South Union Company, are of
opinion, that the Manchester South Union Company deserves the cordial
support of the City of Lichfield, and this Committee pledges itself to
originate a memorial to the Members for the City of Lichfield, and to lay
the same before the inhabitants generally, for the purpose of receiving the
signatures of such as may be favourable to the object proposed, and to use
every other means in their power to promote the objects of the Manchester
South Union Company.

RICHARD GREENE, Chairman.

[17-12-1836]

The notice, laying down as it does the policy of the Railway
Committee, is interesting because it contradicts the myth which
has been fostered for so many years that at Lichfield, as in several
other towns, the Corporation and other interests were concerned
to keep railways out of the town, and for this reason the main line
was eventually built well out of Lichfield, to the general incon-
venience of the inhabitants. As we have just seen, the reverse was
actually the case. At the same time, those of us who live in
Lichfield today cannot help feeling thankful that the Railway
Committee were unsuccessful in their efforts; the idea of a railway
line from Pones Mill passing north of Stowe Pool to a terminus
with a goods yard near Lombard Street is not one that appeals.
In any case, had it been built, it would probably have fallen to the
Beeching axe in the 1950s, and would now be derelict.

The Manchester and South Union Railway Co. was one of
two companies competing for the right to build what later became
known as the Trent Valley line, the other being the Manchester
and Cheshire Junction Railway. In the event, neither was able to
obtain the necessary Parliamentary permission, and so Lichfield
remained without a railway for another decade. As the coaches
faded out the city relapsed into a state of suspended animation.
Trade declined, and the list of bankruptcies over the next few
years makes melancholy reading. Not only that, but with the
passing of the coaches, Lichfield ceased to be a place of resort for
the well-to-do families of the county who in the past had maintained town houses in the city for use during the race weeks and

Yeomanry weeks when the place became a centre of social life. When the railway enabled one to get easily to Buxton, Bath or London, why bother to go to Lichfield for recreation?

Before long the place had lost its air of bustle and had become a quiet market town, almost wholly dependent for its trade on the surrounding farmers and the patronage of the clergy. Business interests were few and on a small scale, and the city was governed by a worthy but unenterprising corporation which left the real work of local government to a body of improvement commissioners while it revelled in picturesque ceremony—processions with sword-bearers and macebearers and civic dinners with loving cups and toasts—excellent things in themselves but no substitute for good local government.

It was another ten years before the plan to put Lichfield on the railway map came to fruition. There had been a second attempt to promote a bill in 1841, this time by a company known as the Stafford & Rugby Railway Co., but this had also been thrown out, opposition from the existing railways being too strong. Finally, in 1844, Sir Robert Peel, M.P. for Tamworth and Prime Minister, took an interest in the project and shepherded a third bill through Parliament. The Trent Valley Railway Bill, as it was known this time, received the Royal Assent on the 21st of July, 1845. Sir Robert Peel cut the first sod on the 13th of November, in a field known as Camel Close on Staffordshire Moor, about half a mile north of Tamworth. Work on the line proceeded steadily for two years and it was opened to the public on the 30th of November, 1847.

To the inhabitants of Lichfield the building of their first line of railway must have been a source of great interest and wonder. No work of this magnitude had taken place in or around the city since the completion of the cathedral over 400 years ago, and this time it heralded the arrival of a new technology, more wonderful even than today's " Spaghetti Junction."

First came the surveyors with their theodolites and chains; then the line of little white pegs which marked the centre of the railway advanced steadily across the countryside. In its wake came the navvies, a legendary race of men who performed prodigious feats of earthmoving as with pick and shovel, wheel-barrow and horse-drawn cart, they opened out cuttings and raised embankments. They worked in gangs, each gang paid so much per cubic yard at a rate which they agreed with the contractor as they went along, according to the type of soil they encountered. They were proud men, independent in character, colourful in their dress, who worked hard, fought hard and drank hard. They were the élite of the railway workmen, lavish in the way they spent their money, the despair of the clergy through whose parishes they passed and the constant worry of mothers of country maidens.

Not so fortunate were the ordinary labourers, who on the Trent Valley line were paid from two shillings to two and sixpence a day of ten hours. Nor were they certain of receiving all of this, as the following letter* from Sir Charles Wolseley to his friend Edward Tootal shows. Tootal was a Manchester businessman, owner of the textile firm which still bears his name, and a director of the Trent Valley Railway Co. The route of the railway lay through Sir Charles Wolseley's estate near Rugeley, but his concern was not only for his property but also for the men working on the line.

" My dear Sir," he wrote to Tootal, " There is shameful work going on on our line of railway, particularly on the score of the Truck System.† Now you know as well as I can tell you, *that* cannot be carried on without the aid of those who are subordinate agents—will you then be kind enough to inform me to whom I am to apply to put a stop to it—there has already been one strike and I know from scores of the workmen that they are naturally dis-satisfied. There are also a strange set of fellows employed as timekeepers—but however only let me get at the proper person to whom I can make the complaint and I shall be satisfied, and I am, my dear sir,

Yours very sincerely,
Charles Wolseley.

P.S.—Will you be so good as to tell me when the workmen begin on my estate, and have to retire from work—how am I to hinder them or more properly, to force them from trespassing on the land contiguous to the line?

---

* British Rail Archives.
† The Truck System was the payment of wages other than in legal tender.

Not all the landowners were so enlightened, however. Most of them were concerned more with the price they could get for their property. There still exists, in the British Rail archives, the collection of letters sent to his superiors by Mr J. J. Berkley, the Resident Engineer for the section of line between Stafford and Tamworth. Evidently the engineering work proceeded much faster than the legal transactions, for again and again we find him informing the company that he is ready to enter a section of the proposed line of railway, only to be held up by an angry owner protesting that he has not yet been paid for his land. Ironically, the most militant of these objectors was the Vicar of Colton who told Mr Berkley that if the engineers dared to enter his land he would lead his own private army against them and " destroy the works."

The line was opened on 30th November, 1847, and so Lichfield acquired its first rail link, and its first railway station. This was situated on the north side of the Burton Road, just below the existing Trent Valley Hotel, (built as an adjunct to the railway).

At this period railway architects still tried to design buildings that were in harmony with their surroundngs, and for the buildings of the Trent Valley Railway the architect, Livock, chose the Tudor Gothic style. All the station buildings and crossing-keepers' cottages were in this fashion, in red brick, the station at Atherstone being one of the few now remaining. The station at Lichfield, which can be seen in the accompanying engraving, was approached by a drive from the Trent Valley Road, and from this side gave a very passable impression of a Tudor country mansion. It continued in use as a dwelling for railway staff after Lichfield Station had been moved to a new position on the south side of the Burton Road, and was used for this purpose until it was demolished in 1971.

The picture is interesting for a number of reasons, giving as it does a good idea of a country railway station of the period. It must have been drawn soon after the opening of the line in 1847, and is a view of the railway looking northward, the bridge in the background being the one which carries the road from Lichfield to Brownsfield Farm and Curborough. The locomotive standing on the down line (to the left of the picture) would appear to be one of Robert Stephenson's standard 2-2-2 passenger locomotives, first built in 1835 and therefore a little old fashioned by the time of the drawing. The train on the other line is composed of the four-wheeled carriages of ten years before. Other period pieces are the curious signal, a type which had gone out of use by 1849, and of course the bonnets and crinolines, top hats and short overcoats, of the waiting passengers.

The reason for the old-fashioned locomotives may well have been the fact that the Trent Valley Railway never had any engines of its own, nor, indeed did it ever operate its own line. In March 1846, while it was still under construction, the directors concluded a deal with the London and Birmingham Railway whereby the latter company purchased the Trent Valley Railway lock, stock and barrel for the sum of £584,000 (paid by cheque).

Four months later the London & Birmingham, the Grand Junction and the Manchester & Birmingham Railways all amalgamated to form the new London & North Western Railway. Thus, by the time the Trent Valley line opened it formed part of the LNWR main line from Euston to Crewe. It was operated by the former London & Birmingham, now the Southern Division of the LNWR, who no doubt kept their newest engines for the London to Birmingham run.

Three times a day in each direction the tall-funnelled loco-motives with their trains of four-wheeled coaches took up and deposited their loads of passengers at Trent Valley station. First class travellers were conveyed the mile from the centre of Lichfield in their own carriages or by cab, while second-class and " Parliamentaries "* were catered for by the horse omnibuses which were run by the George and Swan Hotels.

Lichfield had at last arrived on the railway map. But by now the railway age had been in existence for over ten years, and fortunately or unfortunately (according to one's point of view), while other towns had been forging ahead with the help of the railway, Lichfield had drifted into a state of cosy isolation.

---

* Parliamentary Trains had been introduced in 1844 by W. E. Gladstone when he was President of the Board of Trade. His Act required all railway companies to run at least one train a day in each direction at a speed of not less than twelve miles an hour, at a fare of not more than 1d a mile and in carriages with seats fully protected from the weather.

CHAPTER III

Lichfield and the Railway Mania

The " Railway Mania " of 1845 and 1846 was one of the most extraordinary phenomena of 19th century economic history. We saw in Chapter II how the first trunk railways appeared in the 1830s, and for a time after this development was fairly steady. In 1844 some 800 miles of new railway was sanctioned by Parliament, and then suddenly an orgy of speculation broke out and new railway schemes were being promoted every day. The total mileage approved in 1845 rose to 2,700 and in 1846 it rocketed to 4,500. The reason for this sudden speculation, the like of which had not been seen since the days of the South Sea Bubble, was the spectacular success of George Hudson, the " Railway King," who developed the Midland Railway in such a way as to produce dividends of 10 per cent for his delighted shareholders.

The financial climate was also favourable for speculation, for after several years of economic stagnation trade had improved and money become more abundant. Bank rate was only $2\frac{1}{2}$ per cent, and there was no shortage of promoters eager to follow Hudson's example.

Some of the schemes proposed were doomed from the start. Many of them never got as far as Parliament; others fell an easy prey to the objections of Parliamentary committees, while of those which did succeed in obtaining an act many were unable to raise sufficient capital to complete their lines and either petered out half way or were swallowed up by the larger companies.

The summer of 1845 was a period of feverish activity all over the country as solicitors worked long hours drafting Parliamentary Bills and engineers equally long hours surveying projected lines and drawing up the plans and sections to accompany the bills.

The climax to all this work came in November, when Parliament, already harassed by the extraordinary number of railway bills placed before it, set a deadline beyond which no more bills would be accepted for the current session. The deadline was to be midnight on 30th Novembr, 1845. Immediately there was frenzied activity by all railway promoters to get their bills ready before this time in order to avoid having to wait until the next session. As the deadline drew near the activity rose to a crescendo. Each bill had to be accompanied by plans and sections of the proposed line, and the engineers and surveyors worked twenty-four hours a day, right up to the last moment, while post-chaises stood ready to rush the draft bills and their plans up to London at a moment's notice. Where railways already existed, special trains were booked for the purpose, though not without opposition from the railway company concerned if they suspected that the special train was to be used for the conveyance of a bill for a railway which might eventually be competing against them. In one such case the promoters having been refused carriage by a railway company, placed all the plans and documents in a coffin, dressed up the solicitor's clerks as mutes, and proceeded to London in the guise of a funeral.

As the day of 30th November wore on incredible scenes developed at Westminster as vehicles from all over the country converged on the office of the Clerk responsible for private bills at the House of Commons. By evening there was a jostling crowd of post-chaises, cabs, horsemen and hundreds of clerks, messengers and solicitors, pushing and shoving outside the offices in a desperate attempt to get their bills accepted before the deadline at midnight.

Throughout the country the scene was repeated on a much smaller scale, for the law required that plans of any proposed railway must be deposited with the Clerk of the Peace for every county or borough through which the railway would pass, and the same deadline applied in these cases as well. So it was that on the evening of 30th November, 1845, Charles Simpson, Solicitor and Clerk of the Peace for the City and County of Lichfield sat late in his office to receive any railway plans that might be submitted to him.

Mr Simpson was a Lichfield " Character " throughout most of the 19th century. He was born in 1800 and died in 1890, and apart from his schooldays at Shrewsbury he spent the whole of his life in Lichfield. He was the third generation of the Simpson family to be Town Clerk of Lichfield, succeeding his father in 1825. He was also Coroner and Clerk of the Peace, posts which he held from 1823 until his death. He held very strong Liberal views and was ever in conflict with the Tories. As a result he lost the post of Town Clerk in 1844, when the Tories acquired a majority on the Town Council, only to be reinstated when the Liberals came back in 1849. Thereafter no one dared attempt to remove him until 1887, when he was asked to resign. He refused and his final removal from office was only effected after much litigation, his tenacity and obstinacy bringing him close to imprisonment.

The area of the City and County of Lichfield is some sixteen square miles; not, one would think, space for a great many lines of railway. Already, as mentioned in Chapter II, an Act had been passed for the building of the Trent Valley line to the east of the city and as the deadline of midnight on 30th November drew near plans of railways began to pour in to Mr Simpson's office in St John Street.

The first two arrived on 29th November. One was for a line to be called the Shrewsbury and Leicester Railway which was intended to start at Shrewsbury and come via Penkridge and over Cannock Chase to approach Lichfield via Burntwood and Pipe Hill. After crossing the south side of the city it would proceed via Streethay to join the Trent Valley line at Huddlesford, hoping no doubt to reach Leicester over the tracks of other companies for the rest of the way.

The other was entitled the Macclesfield & Lichfield Railway. It left the Trent Valley Railway a little north of the Lichfield station and skirted the city to the north-east, through Curborough, Alrewas Hay, Hamstall Ridware and on via Blithfield and Leek to Macclesfield, where it joined the Manchester & Birmingham Railway.

On 30th November the first plans of the day came at 2.00 p.m. and were deposited by the promoters of a line to be known as the Trent Valley, Midlands & Grand Junction Railway, the object of which was to link Dudley, Wolverhampton and Walsall with the north-west of England by a line through Lichfield joining the Birmingham & Derby line of the Midland Railway at Wichnor. The joint engineers of the line were Robert Stephenson (son of Old George), Thomas Gooch and George P. Bidder.

As each set of plans arrived Mr Simpson tied them up in pink tape, sealed it, and wrote the date and time of deposit on the outside of the roll, which he then signed.

The next set of plans arrived at 4.30 p.m. They were from the promoters of the Birmingham, Lichfield & Manchester Junction Railway, a line that was to leave the Grand Junction at Aston, on the outskirts of Birmingham, and proceed via Sutton Coldfield to Lichfield, passing to the south of the city and joining the Trent Valley at Streethay. It thus anticipated by about thirty years the present Birmingham to Lichfield line. As Mr Simpson glanced through the plans he noted that they were meticulously drawn and signed by two engineers, George Taylor and John Robinson McClean. The name of McClean meant nothing to Mr Simpson at that time, but it was one which over the next twenty years was to become increasingly familiar to him in his capacity as Town Clerk, and to many other people in and around Lichfield.

As the November evening darkened and the gas lamps were lit outside in the street, the Clerk of the Peace sat at his desk waiting for late arrivals. He had time to finish his dinner before the next visitor arrived at 8.30 p.m. bearing the plans of a railway calling itself the South Staffordshire Junction Railway. Once again the drawing carried the signature of John Robinson McClean, this time in collaboration with a Mr Stileman. The line they had devised began at Dudley and ran via Wednesbury to Walsall; thence to Rushall, Walsall Wood, Ogley Hay, Wall, Lichfield and on to a junction with the Birmingham & Derby Railway. It therefore covered much the same ground as did the Trent Valley, Midland & Grand Junction Railway, the plans of which had been deposited earlier in the day.

By now no less than five railways had been proposed, all deposited within the space of two days and all passing in one direction or another through the city of Lichfield. A vision of a city criss-crossed by railway lines must have been forming in the mind of the Clerk of the Peace as he sat wondering whether any more were on the way.

It was 11.30 p.m. before his question was answered by the arrival of yet another set of plans, this time those of the Birmingham & Manchester Railway. (The connection with Manchester, remote as it was, was presumably stressed to attract investment from that quarter). The engineers this time were George Remington and that distinguished civil engineer, Sir John Rennie, famous as the designer of the new London Bridge of 1832. Their proposed line was yet another which started from a connection with the Grand Junction Railway at Aston and then came to Lichfield via Sutton Coldfield and Shenstone. Just before entering the city it swung north and passed through Leomansley and thence to Handsacre and Rugeley. It terminated at Tean, where presumably it was intended to join the North Staffordshire line from Uttoxeter to Stoke-on-Trent.

These plans, too, were sealed and signed and the Clerk of the Peace sat back and listened for the clock of St Mary's Church to strike midnight. In a few moments his vigil would be ended.

But as he listened the quiet of the night was broken by the sound of galloping horses. A carriage drew up outside his office; doors slammed, voices were raised, footsteps hurried on the steps up from the street and a furious rat-tat-tat sounded from the knocker. Mr Simpson opened the door to the sight of horses steaming in the light of carriage lamps and shadowy figures holding bundles of papers.

They brought the papers inside and laid them on his desk, and explanations and apologies followed. They were the plans of the South Union & Birmingham Junction Railway, straight from their Birmingham drawing office. Some of the drawings were still in pencil with alterations and amendments still visible; the plans

were just as they had come from the drawing board with no attempt
to sort or collate them; all evidence of frantic last-minute work to
beat the deadline.

As he examined them the Clerk of Peace saw that the line they
proposed was yet another connection between the Grand Junction
Railway at Birmingham and the Trent Valley Railway. This time
however, the route lay through Aston, Perry Barr, Aldridge,
Shenstone, Hammerwich, Burntwood, Lichfield (to the north),
Farewell, Armitage and Rugeley.

When at last his visitors had departed, Mr Simpson tied up
and sealed the bundle of plans. On the outside he wrote, " As
deposited with me (all sheets loose) in my office at Lichfield, 30th
November, 1845, a few minutes before midnight."

Then he took down his hat and coat, put out his candles and
walked to his house in Lombard Street.

*   *   *

Mr Simpson need not have worried about the future of
Lichfield. In actual fact, only one of the seven proposed railways
obtained Parliamentary consent, though two others did amalgamate
to obtain eventual approval. The plans of the other four languished
in Mr Simpson's deed boxes, gathering dust, for many years until
a century and a quarter later the writer of this book had the
privilege of breaking the seals and unrolling them once again.
They are an interesting glimpse from the past of what might have
been.

The one line which obtained Parliamentary approval was the
Birmingham, Lichfield & Manchester Junction Railway. It was
stillborn, however, for almost immediately, before a spade had
been turned on the line, the company was taken over by the newly-
formed London North Western and the whole project was put into
cold storage. It was another forty years before Lichfield and
Birmingham were linked directly by rail.

The two which eventually amalgamated were the South
Staffordshire Junction and the Trent Valley, Midland & Grand
Junction. The story of their fight to build their lines, in each case

over much the same route, is typical of the Railway Mania. The fight was carried on with no holds barred, and it was only ended when a Parliamentary shot-gun marriage amalgamated the two concerns in a new company.

The promoters of the South Staffordshire Junction Railway met for the first time at the George Hotel, Walsall, on 10th July, 1845. In the chair was Charles Smith Forster, Esq., of Hampstead Hall, a Walsall banker and High Sheriff of Staffordshire, and the prospectus which was issued contained the names of a provisional committee of forty-five members including a strong contingent of Lichfield notables. There was the Vice-Chairman Richard Croft Chawner, Esq., of Wall, a Lichfield magistrate, who later on was to play a leading part in several engineering schemes in the Lichfield district; General Dyott of Freeford Hall and his son Captain Dick Dyott, representatives of a family having long and historic connections with the City of Lichfield; the Mayor of Lichfield, Thomas Ready; William Holmes, proprietor of a carriage building works in Bore Street; Thomas George Lomax, bookseller and former Mayor of Lichfield; John Mott, J.P. of The Close; John Neville of Haselour Hall and John Delane Griffiths of Whittington. Later they were joined by another local landowner, John Pavier of Hammerwich. Dyott & Son of Lichfield were one of the company's solicitors and Palmer & Greene the local bankers.

" This short but important railway," explained the prospectus, " will commence by forming a junction with the Birmingham & Derby Railway at the viaduct over the River Trent near Alrewas, and will proceed in nearly a straight line to Dudley, being a distance of nearly twenty-one miles, forming a direct and unbroken Railway communication between Derby and the north-midland counties and Worcestershire, Herefordshire and the south-western counties of England.

" This Railway includes in its course the city of Lichfield and the large and rapidly increasing town of Walsall; leaving which it will continue through the manufacturing and mining districts of Wednesbury and Tipton to its terminus at Dudley where it will unite with the railways connecting Stourbridge and Kidderminster, Stourport and Worcester and the whole of the south-west district.

Near Bescot Bridge it will join the Grand Junction Railway so as to form the shortest route to Birmingham, and by means of a branch through Darlaston and Bilston, to join the proposed lines from Birmingham and Dudley, will also form the most direct line to Wolverhampton.

" The shortest and most direct lines will thus be formed for the transit of manufactured iron &c from the centre of the vast mining and manufacturing districts of South Staffordshire to Gainsborough and Hull, and to Sheffield and other great markets of the north.

" The ironstone and other produce of the Derbyshire mines will also be brought by means of this railway direct to the furnaces of Staffordshire, and coal from Cannock Chase and Brown-Hills (the best for domestic purposes) will be conveyed, at small cost, to supply the towns of Walsall, Wolverhampton and Birmingham."

The capital intended to be raised would be £500,000 and this would be divided into 20,000 shares of £25 each.

What the prospectus did not say was that the Grand Junction Railway (soon to become part of the big London North Western amalgamation) was interested in this proposed local line through the Black Country to the extent of expressing its willingness to take up a third of the shares in it. The interest stemmed from the fact that the South Staffordshire line would run right into the country now dominated by George Hudson's Midland Railway, and would give the Grand Junction a foothold in that territory. Empire-building had already become a prominent feature of railway politics.

Nor was this the only instance of railway politics impinging on what had been at first a purely local project. At this time the Battle of the Gauges was raging, between the broad-gauge party which favoured railways built to Isambard Kingdom Brunel's gauge of 7ft 0ins between the rails and the narrow gauge party which plumped for George Stephenson's gauge of 4ft 8½ins.

Now, at Dudley, the proposed line would make a junction with the Oxford, Worcester & Wolverhampton Railway, which was being built as a broad gauge line. Here was an opportunity for the broad-gauge party to push their empire a little further east. and it seems likely that the overtures were made at an early date to the members of the South Staffordshire Junction Provisional Committee, for on the 24th of July we find that body resolving that they approach Mr I. K. Brunel to see if he would accept the position of Engineer to the line. The fact that he declined probably saved them from considerable expense, but even so, that part of the line between Wednesbury and Dudley was built in such a way that it could be used as a mixed-gauge line (for both broad and narrow-gauge trains).

But while the South Staffordshire Junction had been making these plans, their rivals had also been at work. The Provisional Committee of the Trent Valley, Midland & Grand Junction Railway had been formed earlier in the year. Its Chairman was Colonel Anson, son of Lord Lichfield, and among the subscribers were several local people. One of these was Richard Greene, of Stowe House, Lichfield, who, it will be remembered, had been Chairman of the Lichfield Railway Committee of 1836. Another member of that committee was Harvey Wyatt, land agent, of Barton-under-Needwood, who now offered to take £5,280 worth of shares in the T.V.M. & G.J. George Anson, one of Lichfield's two M.P's, and his wife took up another £8,000, while others from the city included in the Schedule of Subscribers were Charles Simpson (Clerk of the Peace and Coroner), £400; Charles Edward Stringer (Painter, of Dam Street),* £300, and John Thorneloe (Clockmaker, Bore Street), £100.

Overshadowing these supporters however, were the big guns such as Henry Tootal, leader of a group of Manchester business men; Edmund Peel, brother of Sir Robert Peel who had been the force behind the Trent Valley Railway, now nearing completion; and the great George Hudson and his colleague John Ellis, Chairman of the Midland Railway. For just as the Grand Junction

---

* C. E. Stringer is remembered for his sketches of Lichfield scenes made in the first quarter of the 19th century. These are now in the Stringer collection in the Bodleian Library, Oxford.

supported the S.S.J., so the Midland looked to the T.V.J.R. to supply them with a route into the Black Country, and accordingly offered to take £72,000 of the shares.

The line which they proposed to build differed somewhat from that of the South Staffordshire Junction. It began at Wolverhampton and followed the route of Wednesfield—New Invention—Bloxwich — Pelsall — Ogley Hay — Hammerwich — Pipe Hill — Lichfield—Alrewas—Wichnor. It thus passed north of Walsall. but a branch line was proposed from Birch Coppice, near Pelsall, to pass through Walsall and Wednesbury to Dudley. The proposed capital was £425,000 in £12 shares, and the engineer was to be Robert Stephenson.

On 14th July, 1845, when the South Staffordshire Junction Provisional Committee were holding their third meeting, they received a delegation from their rivals. It consisted of Richard Greene and Harvey Wyatt, and its purpose was to suggest the expediency of the two companies amalgamating and asking on what terms the S.S.J. would agree to this. The terms that were forthcoming not being agreeable, the T.V.M. & J.R. withdrew their suggestion and from then on each company strove towards the object of getting its own bill through Parliament and at the same time frustrating that of its rival.

Preliminary surveys were carried out to establish the routes to be followed. These did not necessarily clash with each other, for while that of the T.V.M. & G.R. followed the line of railway that exists today between Walsall and Lichfield, the S.S.J. favoured a route via Rushall, Walsall Wood (which really was a wood in those days), Ogley Hay, Sandhills, Wall (Moat Bank) and Lichfield, crossing Upper St John Street by the present King Edward's School and then turning north to cross the Burton Road at Wissage. From here it turned east again and crossed the Trent Valley line at right angles, close to the original station. Near Fradley it crossed back over the Burton Road by the Bull's Head inn to make the junction with the Birmingham and Derby at Wichnor.

While the two Parliamentary Bills were in course of preparation the promoters of each were busy obtaining the consent of the various landowners through whose property the lines were to pass.

At the same time they were approaching anyone who might be affected to sign a petition *against* the bill of their opponents. Many letters such as the following,* addressed to Messrs Dyott & Son, must have passed through the offices of the solicitors concerned.

Brereton

" Dear Sirs,

I return your letter signed as requested. About a fortnight ago a Gent called upon me, he said by direction of George Birch, and wished me to petition against the South Staffordshire Junction Railway, as they were going through my bit of land and had not given notice nor properly described it.

I told him I would do no such thing, as I particularly wished the S.S.J.R. to pass.

I remain,

yours truly,

S. Poole "

But the T.V.M. & G.J. promoters carried out one major coup in connection with their petition. The then Mayor of Lichfield was Thomas Ready who lived in Bore Street and worked the mill in Dam Street. He was a member of the provisional committee of the S.S.J.R. By some extraordinary means (one suspects a bit of " nobbling " in the bar of the George or Swan) he was pursuaded to sign the petition against his own company! It would be interesting to know what his fellow-members said when they heard about this astonishing blunder, but whatever passed the wretched Mayor had to make a speedy recantation. This took the form of a " prayer " to the House of Commons.* It ran :

" SOUTH STAFFORDSHIRE JUNCTION RAILWAY
PETITION OF THE MAYOR OF LICHFIELD, THOMAS READY

————

The humble petition of the undersigned, Thomas Ready, Mayor of Lichfield Sheweth,

* Dyott Collection, County Record Office, Stafford.
* Draft copy in the Dyott Collection, Staffordshire County Record Office.

That bills are now before your Honorable House for making a railway and branches therewith, to be called The South Staffordshire Junction Railway.

That a petition to your Honorable House against the said South Staffordshire Junction Railway was presented to your petitioner in the month of March for signature, by an agent of the promoters of a competing line of railway called the Trent Valley, Midlands and Grand Junction Railway, and on faith of the representations made by the agent to your petitioner, he was induced to sign the said petition.

That your petitioner has since ascertained that the statement made to him was untrue or totally misunderstood by your petitioner and he is therefore desirous of withdrawing from the petition.

Your petitioner therefore humbly prays your Honorable House that the said petition may not be received by your Honorable House as the petition of your petitioner, and if the same is presented to your Honorable House the name of the petitioner be erased therefrom."

Among those who gave evidence before the Parliamentary Committee considering the South Staffordshire Junction Bill were Alderman Lomax and the Vice Chairman, Richard Croft Chawner. The evidence of Mr Lomax has already been mentioned in Chapter II. That of Mr Chawner went as follows:

" The want of general railway accommodation is much felt in Lichfield. The proposed line forms part of a great and comprehensive scheme of railway for the south Staffordshire and Midland districts.

" Walsall, Wednesbury, Tipton, Bilston, Darlaston and Dudley, the various works and the populous places in those localities, are supplied with garden and agricultural produce from Lichfield and the rich lands in that neighbourhood.

" The present mode of conveyance is by carts, which occasions great expense and loss of time. The market gardeners generally leave at 12 o'clock at night and do not return until 5 or 6 the following evening. This occasions a great cost also to the consumer.

" By this line I consider the market gardeners would convey their produce at a considerably less expense and the inter-communication would enable them to send to these places three or four times a day at least.

" The value of land would be much increased and many acres now in other cultivation could be worked for market gardening purposes. Garden land in the proximity of the line at Lichfield lets now for £5 an acre, and I have no doubt would fetch more.

" Many people from all parts of England visit Lichfield, and I have no doubt that if this line were made the increase would be very great.

" A cattle market has been established in Lichfield within the last few years. The situation for the supply is excellent and the proposed line will convey the produce to the best markets. It is held monthly and is fast increasing. This railway will make it one of the best markets in the country."

Faced with a problem akin to that which confronted King Solomon when the two mothers came to him, both claiming the same child, the Parliamentary Committee solved it in much the same way. The line of railway, they decided, should be divided into two parts. The South Staffordshire Junction Company were authorised to build that part which ran between Dudley and Pelsall, and the Trent Valley, Midlands & Grand Junction Company were given the section from Pelsall to Wichnor. And then, on the principle that a nod is as good as a wink to a blind horse, the committee inserted a clause into each of the bills to the effect that the respective companies could, if they had the agreement of three-fifths of their directors, amalgamate with their opposite number to form one company to build the whole line. In this form both bills were passed and received the Royal Assent on the same day, 3rd August, 1846.

A month later each company appointed a delegation of five directors to meet and discuss amalgamation. This time their meeting was successful, and the terms of a settlement were agreed. Each company was to contribute the full amount of its authorised capital, shareholders of the T.V.M. & G.J. were to get one £12 share in the new company for every £20 of their own stock, and those of the S.S.J. three new shares for every one (£25) share of their old company. The name of the new company would be the South Staffordshire Railway Co.

CHAPTER IV

Lichfield's Own Railway

The first meeting of the board of the new company took place on 6th October, 1846. It is indicative of the more influential position of the S.S.J. party that Charles Forster became Chairman, and that one of the first items of business was to appoint John Robinson McClean Engineer to the line. He was to be paid at the rate of £350 for each mile of railway as completed. At the same meeting they appointed John Acton as Book-keeper to the company a˙ a salary of £10 per annum—an interesting commentary on Victorian values.

Work was to commence on the short length of line (about $1\frac{1}{4}$ miles) between Walsall and Bescot, which would allow the South Staffordshire to operate a service between Walsall and Birmingham over the former Grand Junction Railway (now L.N.W.R.). At the same time a start was to be made on the section between Lichfield Trent Valley and Pipe Hill, where the proposed Birmingham, Manchester and Lichfield would make its junction. Soon work was in full swing on the whole of the line between Alrewas and Walsall, 766 men and 111 horses being employed. The men brought their own problems with them, and foreseeing one of these the Board sent donations of £5 each to Birmingham General Hospital and Stafford Infirmary " in order to obtain relief for the Workmen on the line in case of accident." But a letter from the Mayor of Lichfield requesting the company to meet the cost of extra police constables rendered necessary by the number of labourers on the line got a polite refusal and a suggestion that he try taking the matter up with the contractors instead.

At the same meeting the Mayor of Walsall and the Vicar of St Matthew's, Walsall, attended to urge the directors not to run any trains on Sundays. Opposition to Sunday trains was very common at this time; many were the denunciations from pulpits, sometimes couched in very lurid terms about " Excursions to Hell." The Grand Junction Railway, which ran trains on Sundays, published the profit from its Sabbath services separately in its annual accounts, and gave shareholders the opportunity to renounce this portion of their dividend if they so wished, the money to go to charity instead. Many did so, and one example of the resulting good works is Christ Church, Crewe, which was built out of the proceeds of the Grand Junction Sunday Travel Account.

On the South Staffordshire the directors regretted that they could not entertain the suggestion of the Mayor and Vicar of Walsall, and it is interesting to note that no such request came from the cathedral city at the other end of the line. Instead the Dean and Chapter asked that the Sunday trains might be timed to enable them to be used by people attending the cathedral services, and this was done until passenger services were eventually discontinued—an interesting example of the pragmatism that so often distinguishes the Church of England.

Nor does there appear to be any indication that the shareholders of the South Staffordshire Railway ever exhibited reluctance to accept dividends earned by Sunday working, and no Sunday Travel Account ever encumbered Mr Acton's books.

In November 1847 the Board requested their Engineers to report on the cost of providing 4 locomotives, 16 carriages and 300 waggons to use on the line when completed. This shopping list is interesting in that it shows very well the nature of the railway; it was to be first and foremost a mineral line and passengers were a very secondary consideration. This was a complete change from the policy of the early railways of the 1830s. The Grand Junction, the London & Birmingham and the Birmingham & Derby were all projects designed to take the place of stage coaches. The new railway coaches were built to the design of the old stage coaches, even to carrying passengers on the roofs; stations were built like coaching inns and were often named after them.* The traffic of these lines consisted of passengers, their luggage, parcels and the mails—exactly what the road coaches had carried. Goods traffic, especially bulk traffic such as coal was left to the canals to handle. Even as late as 1845 this attitude still persisted, and there is a story, often quoted, of how in that year the Midland Railway, anxious to develop a traffic in coal between the Nottinghamshire coalfield and London, but having no entry into the Metropolis, approached the London & Birmingham Railway to see if they would accommodate the coal trains between Rugby and London. When the request reached Captain Bruyères, Superintendent of the London & Birmingham, in his stately office at Euston, he is reputed to have said, " What! Carry coal by railway! They will be asking us to carry dung next! " The arrangement was made rather grudgingly, but only on condition that the coal came in trucks covered with tarpaulins so as not to offend the susceptibilities of passengers on the London & Birmingham.

None of this was to apply to the South Staffordshire line however, and from the start the carriage of minerals was to be its main purpose. In this policy one suspects, from what happened later, that the influence of the Engineer, John Robinson McClean, was very much in evidence.

In building the railway no very great engineering works were required and the construction was uneventful. The story is sometimes told that when excavating the sandstone cutting east of Lichfield City Station, the blasting required had the effect of damaging the steeple of St. Michael's Church, but the author has been unable to find any confirmation of this. It is true that in 1890 the tower was found to have a crack running the whole height of the structure and well up the steeple, but the report of the architect attributed this to subsidence of the soil.

The Architect to the South Staffordshire Railway was Mr Edward Adams of London, and the station buildings which he produced were all modest creations, in keeping with the character

---

* E.g. Four Ashes station between Wolverhampton and Stafford on the Grand Junction. The public house of that name still exists close by.

of the line. The two principal stations, at Walsall and Lichfield, were built in Tudor style, with tall gables and chimneys. That at Walsall is still to be seen, forming part of the present station. The one at Lichfield is no more, having been demolished in 1882 when the present station was built to accommodate the additional services of the newly-opened line from Birmingham and Sutton Coldfield.

The old South Staffordshire station stood further east of the present one, in what was later the goods yard. It was approached from the city by a path which ran across Levett's Field and up some brick steps in front of the station. These can still be seen, near by the present Fire Station.

At Trent Valley the line crossed over the L.N.W.R. as it does today. But the Trent Valley Station, it will be remembered, was about half a mile north of the crossing point, on the far side of the Burton Road. To allow passengers to transfer to the main line the South Staffordshire had their own station, called Trent Valley Junction. It was situated close to Streethay, just past the present signal box. From it a spur line descended to the low-level station some little distance away. Just how passengers got from one station to the other is not clear—presumably the South Staffordshire trains went down the spur to the low-level station and then came back again, but there is no evidence to support this. Whatever the system used, it came to an end in 1872 when the present Trent Valley Station was opened with high-level and low-level platforms adjoining each other.

The one structure of any architectural pretensions on the line was the bridge which carried the railway over St John Street as it entered Lichfield. This was quite close to the site of one of the mediaeval city gates, and the directors decided to build it in a similar style. The result was important enough for a picture of it to appear, with a description, in the " *Illustrated London News.*" From this it can be seen to have had two "towers," one on either side of the road, and each pierced by a gothic arcade forming a footpath. Between the towers was the " gateway " spanning the road. The whole structure was castellated and emblazoned with coats of arms carved in stone. On either side of the bridge the railway embankment was supported at the top by stone retaining walls; altogether it must have presented quite a convincing representation of a gateway through city walls.

The stone for this bridge was supplied by the Earl of Lichfield from his estate at Shugborough, and the coats of arms were selected by Richard Greene of Stowe House, Lichfield, who also paid the cost of carving them. Mr Greene it will be remembered, was the Chairman of the original Lichfield Railway Committee, and an advocate of railway transport for the city. A partner in the firm of Palmer & Greene, Bankers, he was now a director of the South Staffordshire Railway Company.

The bridge no longer exists in its present form. It was rebuilt in 1882 when the line from Sutton Coldfield to Lichfield was opened and it became necessary to provide two more tracks. Mr Greene's heraldic devices were incorporated in the new bridge, and can still be seen there today. The two larger ones, originally over the centre of the roadway on each side, consist of the three leopards of England on one side and on the other a device representing the seal of the City of Lichfield which shows the cathedral above the bodies of three slain kings. The seal was used as in 1849 the city did not possess a coat of arms.

The smaller devices on the north side are all shields sur- mounted by bishop's mitres. They are those of Bishop Hacket, who rebuilt the cathedral after the Civil War, Bishop Clinton, the Norman bishop who laid out and fortified the city, Bishop Lonsdale who was incumbent of the See in 1849, when the railway bridge was built, and finally Bishop Hayworth, a 15th century divine who was not notable for anything in particular. One wonders why Richard Greene selected him. On the south side the arms are those of four laymen—Colonel Anson, who was Chairman of the Trent Valley, Midland & Grand Junction Railway, Sir Charles Forster, Chairman of the South Staffordshire Junction Railway and later of the South Staffordshire Railway. The other two shields are those of the Dyott family of Freeford (Captain Richard Dyott was a director of the S.S.R.) and the Bagots of Blithfield.

On 1st March, 1849, Captain Wynne, Railways Inspector to the Board of Trade, examined the whole of the line between Wychnor (or Wichnor as successive railway authorities have insisted on calling it to this day) and Bescot, and pronounced it safe for use. On 9th April the official opening took place. The Directors and their guests met at Walsall and boarded a special train. The ensuing proceedings were described as follows in the " Illustrated London News."

" This portion of the line opened on Monday, 9th April. The Directors traversed the line and were met at Lichfield Station by the Mayor (J. P. Dyott, Esq., Jnr.) and Corporation in their robes of office, the High Sheriff and the Officers of the City, preceded by the Mace Bearers with their silver-gilt maces. The party proceeded to the George Hotel where a banquet was provided and upwards of 150 people dined. The Mayor presided and John Mott Esq. officiated as Vice-Chairman. Among the company were the Earl Talbot, Viscount Lewisham M.P., Viscount Anson M.P., Viscount Ingestre, C. S. Forster Esq. (Chairman of the Directors), R. C. Chawner Esq. (Vice-Chairman), R. Greene Esq., H. Wyatt Esq., P. Williams Esq., Captain Dyott, P. Potter Esq. (Directors), J. R. McClean Esq. and J. Stileman Esq. (Engineers), The High Sheriff, Major Majende, Captain Blandy, W. Mott Esq., T. Johnson Esq., Aldermen Lomax, Standley and Higgins.

After the customary loyal toasts, the chairman said the next toast on his list was the toast of the evening. It was ' the health of the Directors of the South Staffordshire Railway, that of their Chairman, Mr Forster, and the success of their undertaking.' Today the first journey upon the line had been accomplished, and he had to congratulate the city and the neighbourhood on possessing this excellent means of communication, valuable alike to the rich man and the poor labourer. By it the poorest artisan from the manufacturing districts of the country—the " Black Country " as it was frequently called—might escape into the green fields and the pure air and recreate his exhausted strength by visiting the agricultural portion. Indeed, he hoped to see the miner of Bilston and the artisan of Wednesbury with as ruddy countenances as the peasantry living on Cannock Chase (applause). Indeed, this county, where every article of iron was manufactured from a cannon ball to a half inch nail, might be considered the California of England (applause), and all it needed was the means of sending forth its production which this railway would greatly afford. However, he wished not to run his engine past the station of discretion (laughter), and therefore he at once gave them the health of the Directors of the South Staffordshire Railway.'

C. S. Forster, Esq., in acknowledging the toast, noticed that the line brought into communication the town of Burton, the city of Lichfield and the town of Walsall and adverted to the mutual advantage which must arise. He also referred to the long-neglected but well-known quotation from Dr Darwin:

> ' Soon shall thy arm, unconquered steam, afar,
> Drag the slow barge or drive the rapid car,
> Or on wide-waving wings expanded bear,
> The flying chariot thro' the fields of air.'

and remarked that with a prescience truly wonderful, the Lichfield poet had ventured on a prediction which was now fulfilled within the walls of his own city to the very letter, (applause).

The Chairman then proposed ' the Members for South Staffordshire,' for which Lord Lewisham returned thanks, and concluded by proposing the health of the excellent chairman, the Mayor of Lichfield, which was drunk three times three. The ' Member for the City of Lichfield,' the ' Health of Earl Talbot ' and ' The Corporation of Lichfield ' were the next toasts.

Captain Dyott, after noticing at some length the advantages likely to arise to the district through which the railway passed, and stating that unlike the Trent Valley, which owed its parentage to Manchester, and was brought to birth by a celebrated nurse at Tamworth who turned the first sod, the present line owed its existence to local patronage and support, proposed the healths of Messrs McClean and Stileman the Engineers, and the officers of the Company.

After several other toasts had been drunk, the Mayor quitted the chair and the meeting, which seemed to afford much gratification to every one, broke up about seven o'clock.

Later in the evening a ball was held in the Guildhall, and in due course the special train returned to Walsall with the tired but gratified directors and their guests. So ended a typical opening ceremony such as our Victorian ancestors delighted to put on for the successful completion of a railway or other project. We cannot but admire their stamina in conducting such occasions.

Trains now began to run between Walsall and Burton, and after January, 1850, between Birmingham and Burton. There were only four trains in each direction, and some stations did not have even this—Hammerwich, for example, had only two trains a day except on Tuesdays, when there was a third train from Walsall in the evening. (Tuesday was, and still is, Market Day in Walsall).

No doubt the reason for these few trains was the shortage of engines and rolling stock. For the opening of the line the Company had ordered four passenger and two goods engines from the Manchester firm of William Fairbairn & Co, twelve months before they were required. But as a result of the Railway Mania, Fairbairns, like every other locomotive builder, were overwhelmed with orders. A month before the opening date the engines had still not arrived, and in a panic the directors ordered another three " off the peg " from Sharpe Bros., another Manchester firm. These did not arrive until after the opening either, and so on the great day the South Staffordshire Railway had to borrow its motive power from the London North Western.

When the four passenger engines eventually arrived from Fairbairns they were numbered 1 to 4 and given the names DUDLEY, WALSALL, WEDNESBURY and LICHFIELD. Altogether, in its short history, the South Staffordshire Railway had twenty-nine locomotives. All of them had names and as the list at the end of the chapter shows, most of them were named after places on or near the line. The only stations that did not get a mention in this way were Rushall and Hammerwich—perhaps the latter was too long to get on the side of an engine!

In passing, it may be pertinent to mention that no less than four locomotives in turn carried the name of Lichfield on the London North Western Railway. The Fairburn engine just mentioned was taken over by the L.N.W.R. in 1862 and ran until scrapped twelve years later. Then in 1888 a new engine of Mr Webbs " Dreadnought " Class was given the name CITY OF LICHFIELD, and at the end of its life the title was passed on to an " Experiment " Class locomotive built by Mr Whale in 1906. Finally, in 1952, British Railways, the successors of the L.N.W.R., gave the name to one of their " Pacific " type engines the name-plates of which now rest in Lichfield Museum.

Passenger accommodation on the South Staffordshire line was also very limited to start with. The railway began its life with two first-class carriages, purchased from Messrs Wrights of Saltley for £365 each, six second-class carriages costing £250 each and six composite first and second-class vehicles. There were also six third-class or " Parliamentary " carriages at £205 each, and to complete the inventory there were four luggage vans, two horse boxes and two carriage trucks. These last were for the rather grand people who travelled with their own horses and carriages. Presumably there were not many of this class around Lichfield and Walsall.

At the other end of the scale the S.S.R., shortly after opening, added *fourth* class carriages to their trains. These were open coaches (one can be seen at the rear of the train in the picture of the bridge over St John Street). Mr Hamilton Ellis, in his book " Railway Carriages of the British Isles," describes these as follows:

" The illustration shows another specimen (of fourth-class carriage) from the South Staffordshire Railway, 20ft. long, 7ft. 6in. wide, with 3ft. 9in. sides, and carried on six wheels. The diagram is from a drawing found among old records of the London & North Western Railway which leased the S.S.R. in 1861. Written on the original is a note mentioning that hundreds of holes were bored in the floor to provide updraught and to prevent the passengers' lower extremities from being too warm. The holes served also for the escape of rainwater in bad weather."

Even with their fourth-class carriages the S.S.R. were sorely pressed for passenger accommodation on special occasions. One of these was the Whit Monday Bower, which, as a result of extensive advertising by the railway company attracted huge crowds from the Black Country (as it still does today). Mr G. P. Neale, the first Chief Clerk of the S.S.R., who later became Superintendent of the Line on the L.N.W.R., described in his " Reminiscences " the problems that ensued.

" The number of our carriages was but small, and on the occasion of the Whitsuntide gathering at Lichfield, called ' Lichfield Bower '—a survival of a mediaeval pageant—we ventured on the very risky plan of using open wagons with plank seats, but the experiment was not repeated: cattle trucks were next tried but as the rising generation took to ' mooing ' at the passengers while the train was stationary, the dislike to using such vehicles, even at the low rate adopted, caused the plan to be withdrawn. We exploited Lichfield extensively, using its Cathedral as the attraction; excursion trains both for adults and school children were well supported."

Another spot in Lichfield frequented by Sunday school outings and similar excursions was Borrowcop Hill, to the south of the city. Here, at the spot marked by the 18th century gazebo, is reputedly the site where three Saxon Kings were slain in battle; their dismembered bodies appear on the seal of Lichfield Corporation. This heraldic device appears to have held quite an attraction for the Directors of the S.S.R., for not only did they incorporate it in the decoration of the bridge over St John Street, but they also used it in the combination of shields that graced the sides of the first-class carriages—a form of decoration that called forth plenty of ribald remarks at a time when railway accidents were more common than they are today.

Less than six months after its opening the Directors of the S.S.R. received a proposal to lease the line. It came, surprisingly, from the engineer who had built it—Mr John Robinson McClean, and he offered the company a rent of two per cent on the fixed capital for the first year and thereafter four per cent per annum. Attracted by the idea of sitting back and collecting their rent without any of the responsibility of running the railway, the Directors agreed, and after some canvassing the Shareholders, persuaded by the prospect of a regular dividend on their investment, also gave their consent. This was the first occasion in history that a railway had been leased to a private individual, and before it could be put into effect an Act of Parliament was required . This was duly obtained (13 & 14 Vic., Cap. 58) and on the 21st January, 1850 the lease became effective. After the Board Meeting in Birmingham at which the agreement, for a 21 year lease, was signed, Mr McClean entertained the Directors to dinner in an atmosphere of the greatest cordiality. Not all the members of the Board, however, understood what they had agreed to, and in particular paragraph 6 of the agreement which stated, " The Company to maintain and guarantee to the lessee the enjoyment of all powers, whether under Statutory authority or private contract, at present enjoyed by the Company." At their next meeting the Board issued some instruction to Mr McClean regarding the running of the railway. His reply was short and to the point. " Gentlemen," he wrote, " I must remind you that I am now the Boss."

Whatever the misconceptions of the South Staffs. Directors there were no doubts whatsoever in the mind of John Robinson McClean as to his course of action. A man of restless enterprise, he had entered into the lease of the railway with certain very definite aims in view. One of these was the exploitation of the coalfield which lay to the north of the line, in the area of Cannock Chase. Coal had been mined here in small quantities for centuries, but now the Marquess of Anglesey, the principal landowner in the area, whose seat was at Beaudesert in the middle of the Chase, had started to develop the coalfield further by sinking a pit in the parish of Hammerwich to discover what came to be known as the Cannock Chase Deep Coals.

McClean approached the Marquess with a proposition to form a joint stock company to mine this coal on a large scale. The proposition was favourably received, and as a result the Cannock Chase Colliery Company was formed. The Marquess joined the Board, as also did his son, Lord Alfred Paget and other members were McClean and his friend and business associate of railway days, Mr Richard Chawner who now lived at The Abnalls, Lichfield.

Cannock Chase Number 2 Pit was sunk on the north-east side of Norton Pool (now known as Chasewater). Close by were built the offices of the Company, and from the pit a single-track mineral railway ran across the common to join the South Staffordshire Railway at Anglesey Sidings, half-way between Brownhills and Hammerwich stations. Thus Mr McClean profited from the Cannock Chase coal and at the same time secured traffic for his railway. To haul the trains of coal trucks down to Anglesey Sidings and bring the empties back, the Colliery company purchased in 1856 from Messers Beyer Peacock & Co. of Manchester an 0-4-2 saddle tank locomotive which, not surprisingly, was named McCLEAN.

As the company extended their operations, another six pits were opened in various parts of the Chase, and at the same time the little single-track railway straggled all over the area, from pit to pit. To carry the increased loads another locomotive was ordered from Beyer Peacock & Co. in 1861. Similar to McCLEAN, because that engine had proved so satisfactory, it was named ALFRED PAGET, and in the years that followed it was joined by another four. In 1864 came CHAWNER, in 1867 BROWN, in 1872 ANGLESEY and finally—in 1946!—FOGGO. This was a completely new engine, built in the Company's workshops with parts supplied by Beyer Peacock, but identical with the originals, so satisfactory was the ninety year-old design. McCLEAN, incidentally, lasted until 1956, just 100 years, before being broken up.

Close by Number 2 Pit and the headquarters of the Company, a new town started to grow in what had been bare heathland. Essentially a mining community, it was given the name of Chasetown and rapidly outgrew the little hamlet of Burntwood in which parish it was situated. In 1865 Mr McClean, feeling that Chasetown should have a church of its own, built at his own expense the Parish Church of St Anne. (St Anne is the Patron Saint of miners).

St Anne's is utterly unlike any other church in this part of the country. McClean was a man who had travelled widely, had his own views on architecture and took a direct interest in the building of the church. His architect was Edward Adams, who had worked with McClean for the South Staffordshire Railway, and also for the South Staffordshire Waterworks Company. Outside it is a fairly unassuming building in red brick; inside the idiom is one described in a contemporary account as " Lombardo-Venetian." The wide nave is separated from the side aisles by arcades of rounded arches with jagged cut-brick decoration, carried on circular brick columns with Romanesque capitals. There is much polychrome brickwork, and originally the whole of the interior was decorated liberally with gilding and colouring. The chancel is in the form of an apse, the walls of which are inlaid with various marbles. The founder of the church is commemorated by a tablet at the west end, inscribed as follows: —

In Memory of
JOHN ROBINSON McCLEAN
Member of Parliament
for East Staffordshire
Fellow of the Royal Society
Sometime President
of the Institution of Civil Engineers
The Founder of this Church
and benefactor of this district

Died 13th July, 1873

Aged 60

In the south-west corner there is also a bust of Mr McClean.

The consecration of the church by the Lord Bishop of Lichfield took place on Thursday, the 14th of September, 1865. At the time, the British Association for the Advancement of Science, of which McClean was a member, was meeting in Birmingham. All his fellow-members were invited to the ceremony and to the luncheon which followed in tents adjoining the church. To convey them, Mr McClean laid on a special train from Dudley, over the South Staffordshire Railway. At Anglesey Sidings the carriages were shunted off the main line and hauled by McCLEAN up the mineral track across the common to a temporary platform which had been built by the church.

St Annes claims the reputation of being the first church in Britain to be lit by electricity. As early as 1883 it was fitted with " electriliers " or light fittings using the Edison-Swan system (i.e., carbon filament lamps). These were supplied with current from a dynamo at Number 2 Pit, a few hundred yards away, the supply line consisting of two old iron-rope winding cables, laid in wooden troughs filled with pitch. A piece of one of these cables can still be seen at the church. This novel form of lighting excited much curiosity at the time. Mr McClean one feels sure, would have approved, had he lived to see it.

To return to the South Staffordshire Railway; its life as an independent company was short. The coal traffic brought it prosperity; in 1858 a new branch was opened through Norton Canes to handle the traffic from the collieries being developed there, and in the same year the line from Walsall to Cannock was opened. The London North Western realised that it would add an important part to their network. They approached the South Staffordshire Company with a view to taking it over, and agreement was eventually reached in 1861. The L.N.W.R. were to take possession of the line on the 4th February, Mr McClean being paid £110,099 for the unexpired portion of his lease and the shareholders of the S.S.R. receiving interest on their capital of $4\frac{1}{2}\%$ up to 1871, and thereafter at 4%. So passed the South Staffordshire Railway as an independent body, and the line became part of the great L.N.W.R. complex.

SOUTH STAFFORDSHIRE ENGINE STOCK

No.	Name	Built
1	*Dudley*	1849
2	*Walsall*	1849
3	*Wednesbury*	1849
4	*Lichfield*	1849
5	*Burton*	1849
6	*Stafford*	1849
7	*Bescot*	1845
8	*Birmingham*	1845-50
9	*Wolverhampton*	1845-50
10	*Belvidere*	1845-50
11	*Angerstein*	1850
12	*Pelsall*	1851
13	*Alrewas*	1851
14	*Sylph*	1852
15	*Safety*	1852
16	*Viper*	1852-53
17	*Stag*	1852-53
18	*Esk*	1853
19	*Justin*	1853
20	*Priam*	1853-55
21	*Ajax*	1855
22	*Bilston*	1855-57
23	*Derby*	1855-57

CHAPTER V

The Changing Face of Lichfield

Life is changing all the time, but sometimes so imperceptably that it takes an event such as the passing of some great public figure to bring it home to people that they are moving out of one epoch into another. In our own time the death of Winston Churchill was just such an event; in 1854 the people of Lichfield must have experienced the same feelings when a famous man who had become a legend in his lifetime passed from their midst.

Friday, 5th May, 1854, was a very special day in the history of Lichfield. Throughout the city flags flew at half-mast; shops put up their shutters and people began to gather in the streets. A sense of occasion prevailed. In the afternoon a detachment of 200 men of the 1st King's Own Staffordshire Militia marched into Bird Street with their Colours draped in black and halted outside the George Hotel.

At Trent Valley Station a group of carriages gathered in the forecourt soon after four o'clock. With them was a string of six black horses, their coats shining, their harness immaculate and black ostrich feathers nodding on their heads.

At half-past four precisely a special train drew into the station, at its head one of Mr McConnell's new " Bloomer "* locomotives, its brasswork and bright red paint shining.   Behind it was a train of first-class carriages containing passengers wearing the garments of deep mourning that custom dictated at that time, and imme-diately behind the engine the Great Northern Railway's special funeral car, a flat truck on which was carried a splendid hearse containing a coffin draped in a velvet pall.

The funeral car was uncoupled and shunted into the carriage-loading bay, and porters man-handled the hearse off the car and into the forecourt.   The six horses were harnessed up and the procession set off into the city.

For the first half-mile they passed through fields, for the city did not extend so far in those days.   The first building they came to was the Union Workhouse,* where the Master and Matron, Mr and Mrs Pennal, and their Staff stood outside to pay their respects. On past St Michael's Church on Greenhill went the cortege, down into the city past the shuttered shops and the silent crowds, while the bells of St Mary's and the Cathedral sounded their half-muffled peals.   At the top of Bore Street they turned right into Bird Street and halted outside the George Hotel, where the guard of honour of the Staffordshire Militia presented arms and dipped their Colours.

The coffin was carried into the hotel and placed on a catafalque which had been prepared in the Assembly Room, flanked by four large silver candlesticks.   When all was ready the waiting crowds were admitted, and during the course of the evening several thousand people filed past to pay their respects.

---

* Mrs Amelia Bloomer, an American lady, was famous at this time as the inventor of a type of trouser for women, which came down to the knees, thus displaying the lower parts of the legs.   These were known as " Bloomers." The name was also given by the drivers to their locomotives because the absence of splashers allowed the greater part of the driving wheels to be seen.

* Now St Michael's Hospital.

The coffin itself was covered in crimson Genoa velvet, studded
with gold nails and furnished with gold fittings.   The plate on it
was inscribed as follows:

The Most Honourable
HENRY WILLIAM PAGET
First Marquess of Anglesey,
Earl of Uxbridge,
Baron Paget of Beaudesert,
Field Marshal,
Colonel of the Royal Horseguards,
Lord Lieutenant and Custos Rotuloram
of the Counties of Anglesey and
Stafford,
Constable of Caernarvon Castle,
Vice-Admiral of the coast of North Wales and
Carmarthenshire.
Captain of Cowes Castle
Privy Councillor,
K.G., G.C.B., K.St.P., G.C.H.,
Knight of Maria Theresa of Austria,
Knight of St George of Russia,
Knight of William of Holland

But to most of those who read the inscription he would be
remembered as " One-Leg Paget " or " Old One-Leg," and the
older ones would recall another occasion in Lichfield, nearly forty
years ago when he had entered the city in triumph as one of the
heroes of Waterloo. His subsequent career had included offices as
Master General of the Ordinance, twice Lord Lieutenant of Ireland
and one of the first Chairmen of the Board of Education. His life,
which began twenty years before the French Revolution, lasted well
into the reign of Victoria, to the era of railways and steamships
and the electric telegraph. In its obituary notice the *Times* said
of him, " He belonged to a race of nobles who have passed away
from amongst us, and we shall know them no more . . . If he did
not act the highest part in the world's history, all he did he did
well, and that throughout well-nigh four score years and ten.

Wherever the news of his death is told all will be sorry that ' old Lord Anglesey is gone at last,' and have a kind word and a kind thought for his memory. With him the old race of nobles is well-nigh burnt out."

The next morning the funeral procession assembled once again outside the George and led by a military band playing the Dead March proceeded up Bird Street to the Close. The route was lined with soldiers from his regiments, the bells of the city churches tolled, and all Lichfield was in mourning. In the Cathedral a vast body of mourners filled the nave for the funeral service, after which the coffin was taken to the family vault below the Sacristy.

To most of Lichfield people it must have seemed that the old order was changing. They had said goodbye to one of the old land-owning aristocracy whom they had known as the Lord of the Manor of Longdon; a man who had raised a Regiment of the British Army from among his tenants, a hero of Waterloo whom the Prince Regent had come to visit at Beaudesert to commiserate with him on the loss of a leg in the battle. He was a Whig of the old school who for years had played a prominent part in local politics, and his going was the end of an epoch. And as if to underline the change, his son and heir, the new Marquess, was a director of a joint stock company, registered under the new Companies Act, which was busily engaged in mining for coal under the ancestral estates.

The face of Lichfield was indeed changing, but in fact the change had begun some years before. Whereas in the previous century development in the city had consisted of private houses and shops, in the middle of the nineteenth century it was nearly all in the form of public buildings and works.

The first of these was the new Union Workhouse—a landmark in social history brought about by the Poor Law Act of 1834. Before this time the relief of the poor had been the responsibility of the parishes, each of which had an " Overseer of the Poor " appointed annually at the Vestry Meeting. Parishes varied considerably in the way they met this responsibility. In Lichfield

all three churches had their workhouses—St Mary's in Sandford
Street by the bridge, St Michael's in Greenhill and St Chad's in
Stowe Street. While life in these institutions was no bed of roses,
it was not subject to the rigorous regime that was later to be the
pattern of workhouse existence; nor were the inmates separated
from the rest of the community. Things were changing, however,
and the 1834 Act abolished parish workhouses and in their stead
set up Union Workhouses which served a large number of parishes.
One of these unions was centred on Lichfield, and the " *Staffordshire Examiner* " for 21st December, 1836 (the same issue that
carried the advertisement of the Railway Committee) had also the
following notices:

> " To the Magistrates of the District, and the Gentlemen who
> may be appointed as the Board of Guardians of the Lichfield
> Union.
>
> Gentlemen,
>
> I beg most respectfully to announce my intention of offering
> myself as candidate for the situation of CLERK to your
> Board, and to solicit your support and interest on the day
> of election; assuring you that should I have the honour of
> receiving the appointment it will be my endeavour, by
> unremitting attention to the duties of the office, to discharge
> them to the satisfaction of the Guardians and the public
> generally.
>
> I shall take the earliest opportunity of paying my
> personal respects to the Magistrates of the District, and to
> the Gentlemen who may be elected as the Board of
> Guardians. In the meantime, I beg to subscribe myself,
>
> Gentlemen,
>
> Your most obedient servant,
>
> Edward Allen, Solicitor."

A similar notice appeared over the signature of Francis
Eggington Sen., Vestry Clerk of St Mary's, and after these came
the solicitations of those seeking the post of Relieving Officer.

The Overseer of the Poor for St Mary's Parish was one of these. His appeal read as follows:

" LICHFIELD UNION

To the Magistrates, Owners of Property and Rate Payers within the proposed Union,

Gentlemen,

The Poor Law Commissioners having decided upon forming a Union in this District, I beg to offer myself as a candidate for the situation of RELIEVING OFFICER to the Board of Guardians, and beg to assure them, should I be favoured with their support, it shall ever be my endeavour to show that their confidence has not been misplaced . . .

I am, Gentlemen,

With great respect,

Your most obedient servant,

RICHARD TAYLOR

Overseer of St Mary's Parish."

It is pleasant to think that there actually was a time when the ratepayers of Lichfield were addressed as " Gentlemen " with " great respect," by their " obedient servant "!

The new Board of Guardians met for the first time on 3rd February, 1837. Mr Grove was their Chairman, and among the members of the Board were such familiar names as Richard Chawner, Richard Greene and William Dyott as well as several of the clergy of Lichfield. They began by appointing Philip Dyott, solicitor, as their clerk and then went on to make other appointments. In the place of the former " Overseers of the Poor " they appointed three " Relieving Officers "—John Hewitt, Daniel Proudman and John Woodcock at salaries of £100 per annum each. Another very interesting appointment made at this meeting was that of Henry Gray as " Registrar of Births and Deaths." The modern system of registering every person in the community as they enter or leave this world began in 1837, and for many years the staff who carried this out came under the control of Boards of

Guardians. Notice that there was no mention as yet of marriage
in their title. This was still the province of the church, and though
Registrars had to record marriages, they could not yet perform
them.

To begin with the Guardians had to administer the former
parish workhouses that they took over, but one of their first
important resolutions was to build a new, central Union Workhouse. They decided on a " site opposite St Michael's Church on
Greenhill," and advertised for architect's plans. Of those received,
the plans of Thomas Johnson on the one hand and those of Messers
Moffat and Scott on the other, were considered " the most eligible."

Thomas Johnson was a Lichfield architect, well-known in the
district for his churches. He rebuilt St Michael's Church in 1842
and built Christ Church in 1846. Outside Lichfield his work can
be seen at Bilston, Darlaston, Outer Longton, Upper Tean, Norton
Canes, Leigh and Great Wyrley. He was an expert exponent of
the Victorian Gothic revival long before it had been taken up by
most architects. Later on his son went into partnership with him
and one of their works was the Corn Exchange in Lichfield Market
Place.

Moffat & Scott on the other hand, were little known. They
were both young men, just qualified and building up a practice.
The Poor Law Act of 1834 had been their chance. Having studied
this particular requirement (i.e., the building of workhouses) they
made themselves expert at it. They had plans of workhouses
available at a moments notice, ready to be taken off the shelf, so
that if one of them saw an advertisement by a new Poor Law Union
he would be on the next coach to that place with his plans under
his arm.

Thomas Johnson estimated the cost of carrying out his plans
at £3,000 and Moffat & Scott theirs at £3,090, so there was not
much in it. Then, as often happens on committees, the Lichfield
Guardians split down the middle and divided into two camps, one
in favour of Johnson and the other for Moffat & Scott. From
February, 1837 until September, 1838 they had actually decided
to let Johnson do it, but at the following meeting, when presumably

some absentees had been rounded up, Richard Greene moved an amendment that it should go to Moffat & Scott. It was carried by one vote. Not to be outdone, at the next meeting someone moved that another Lichfield architect, Joseph Potter, should be given a chance and this was carried. Finally it was agreed that the plans should be sent to the Poor Law Commissioners for arbitration, and the Commissioners plumped for Scott & Moffat. Johnson, who had had his plans sent back to him several times for re-drafting, was justifiably annoyed and pressed the Guardians for £150 for work done. He got his money.

So it was that young George Gilbert Scott came to Lichfield for the first time in the exercise of his profession. The result can be seen today in the form of the front part of St Michael's Hospital, an essay in the Tudor style that was so popular at the time. The result is not unpleasing, though the little cupola on the main block seems somewhat out of character and not at all in the Scott tradition. Was it perhaps the idea of one of the Guardians?

The Workhouse was not Scott's last work in Lichfield. Eighteen years later he came again, this time as Sir Gilbert Scott the eminent church architect and one of the chief exponents of what came to be known as " High Victorian Gothic." On this second occasion the subject of his attentions was Lichfield Cathedral, and as a result of his endeavours there he left an almost indelible stamp on that stately pile, a stamp that will be a subject of controversy for centuries to come. But that story belongs to another chapter.

In December the Guardians accepted the tender of a Mr Sissons to construct the building, for the sum of £2,939. It is interesting to note that the bricks were to be made on the site from the clay got out in preparing the foundations.* The only ones purchased were 4,000 blue bricks for the diapering (the diagonal criss-cross patterns on the outside of the brickwork). Unskilled labour was also supplied on the site by any able-bodied paupers who were available.

---

* This was a common practice at the time, where there were suitable deposits of clay, as is the case in the Wissage area of Lichfield.

Work got under way in the new year and on 24th May, 1838, the first stone was ceremoniously laid by the Chairman, Mr Grove, with a silver trowel presented to him by the Mayor of Lichfield. Following the ceremony the Guardians adjourned to the Old Crown inn for luncheon at 3 o'clock, the normal time for such a meal in those days.

The accommodation in the new workhouse was to be for 200 paupers. These would be of all ages, for at one end of the scale children would be born there, mainly the offspring of unmarried mothers. Here, too, would be brought children who had been abandoned or who had lost their parents, to be brought up in the Workhouse until they were old enough to be sent out into the world. At the other end of the scale were those who were past the ability to fend for themselves and came into the Workhouse to end their days. In between these two extremes were men and women of all ages who from ill-fortune, idleness or physical or mental incapacity could not or would not support themselves outside. Sometimes there were whole families, and all the time there were the " casuals," the tramps and tinkers and persons of no abode on the move around the country. The accommodation for 200 would appear to have been more than enough; in the census return for 1841 a total of 92 inmates were present on the night of 31st March. The staff in residence consisted of the Master, the Matron, a Schoolmistress and a Porter. Probably there would be others who lived out.

The minute book of the Guardians* provides an interesting light on the conditions of life in Lichfield Workhouse. Much has been written about the harshness of the Victorian workhouse, and most people's ideas today are based on the writings of Charles Dickens. But in " Oliver Twist " Dickens was describing the old parish workhouse which, as we have seen, was already on the way out when Victoria came to the throne. Materially, it is likely that most of the inmates of Lichfield Workhouse were far better off than they would be in their own homes, at a time when many working people still lived in hovels. The new building provided adequate shelter, heated in winter, and sufficient space per person.

---

* County Record Office, Stafford.

There was a supply of clean water for drinking and washing, and proper sanitation, for the Guardians insisted on water closets being fitted, including separate ones to each dormitory. (These the Master was instructed to lock each morning when the inmates got up and unlock them again when they went to bed). The dormitories were furnished with iron bedsteads, purchased at a cost of thirty shillings each; mattresses were either flock or straw filled and both blankets and sheets were provided. The inmates were clothed in standard workhouse clothing; tenders accepted for this in 1837 included men's shoes (kip or cow leather) at 8/3d (41½p) per pair; womens' black grain ditto at 5/- (25p) per pair, and chldren's at 4/- (20p) per pair. Men's fustian jackets were purchased at 15/- each ((75p), waistcoats at 5/6d (27½p) and trowers (sic) at 8/- (40p) a pair. Undergarments and all the women's and children's clothes were made in the sewing room of the workhouse—in fact the policy was to make the whole institution as self-supporting as possible.

Tenders for foodstuffs also make interesting reading. In the same year the tender for beef at 5½d (2¾p) a pound was to consist of " kernal pieces,* sticking pieces,* neck ends, brisket and one shoulder piece in each weighing." Other commodities bought were skimmed milk at 1d per quart; oatmeal at 1/8d (8½p) a peck; butter at 1/1d (5½p) a pound; sugar at 6½d (2.2p) per pound; coals at 13/4d (46½p) a ton and yellow soap at 5d (2p) a pound.

Following the policy of self-sufficiency the workhouse had to produce all its own vegetables. Unfortunately no diet sheets have survived to show how much each inmate received, but various items in the minutes give some indication of the meals, e.g., " 30/6/38. Ordered that men and women paupers in the work-house be allowed one pint of beer with their cheese meals and that on Mondays and Fridays potatoes be used at Dinner and bread at Supper, and if potatoes be used at Supper they be mashed with milk."

" 13/7/38. The sum of £5 18s 11½d be allocated for regaling the paupers in the workhouse on Coronation Day."

---

* These cuts appear to be unknown to modern home economists.

" 10/2/40. Ordered that the paupers in the workhouse be allowed Roast Beef, Plum Pudding and a pint of Ale for their dinner on the occasion of the Queen's marriage."

The same menu was always provided on the proverbial " Christmas Day in the Workhouse."

In return for these material benefits paupers had to work, and work hard. In addition to the work of the institution itself—the cooking and gardening, the sewing and mending and all the scrubbing done with those pounds of yellow soap—there were certain standard tasks. Before the new workhouse opened on the 8th May, 1840, the Guardians had decided that this work would consist of stonebreaking and oakum picking. A move to install a treadmill in the new building was defeated by 16 votes to 13.

But the whole psychology of the Victorian workhouse was based on the idea that life inside it should be such that those who came in should be anxious to get out as soon as possible, and would not be in any hurry to return. So workhouses were surrounded by high walls, as if to emphasise that their inmates were cut off from society, and the walls were topped with a row of iron spikes—for which reason the workhouse was known to anyone who had any connection with it as " The Spike." The only contact with life outside was the weekly trip on Sundays to St Michael's Church across the road, where the paupers sat in seats specially reserved for them. Always the emphasis was on the debt owed to society which thus cared for their material needs, and the need to adopt the philosophy of self-help so dear to Victorian hearts. As a result there was a stigma attached to anyone who had to use the poorhouse, a stigma which can still be found among old people today. For anyone who had any self-respect, the acceptance of poor relief was a last resort, and many paid a penny a week into a burial club, to ensure that at the last they did not receive a pauper's funeral.

At Lichfield, in the 1840's, this melancholy service was provided by Mr Bonell, a carpenter who lived in Gaia Lane. His tender to the Board of Guardians, dated 7th February, 1837, read as follows: " Coffins, children under seven, 8/- (40 pence) each;

for children seven to fourteen, 12/- (60 pence) each; adults, 16/- (80 pence) each. Shrouds, 2/- (10 pence) each. Tops and bottoms to be of $\frac{3}{4}$ inch timber, sides of $\frac{1}{2}$ inch.

It will be seen from this that a pauper's funeral was of the very simplest kind. Unfortunately, in many places, it was conducted with a complete lack of reverence or concern. Not, one is pleased to note, in Lichfield, for early in the minute book of the Guardians is the record of a letter received from the Rector of St Michael's Church, complaining of the rudeness and lack of feeling of Mr Bonell towards the relatives of a pauper whom he had recently buried. Mr Bonell was called before the Guardians at their next meeting and was told to mend his ways if he wished to keep the contract. This was in keeping with the general outlook of the Lichfield Guardians, for whatever may have happened elsewhere, one gets the impression, reading through their minutes, that they took their responsibilities seriously, and, in the context of people's attitudes at this time, had a general concern for the welfare of those in their care, as well as a thought for economy in the public money they spent.

The Victorian workhouse introduced order into a system which had often been haphazard, slovenly and inefficient. It provided a basic minimum below which no one need slip. But in doing so it lost no opportunity of impressing on those who used it their obligation to society, and in consequence the stigma of " poor relief " has lasted almost to this day.

The impact made on Lichfield by the arrival of the railway has already been mentioned. About the same time that the Trent Valley and City stations were being built, the Conduit Lands Trustees were building the Guildhall in Bore Street. The old structure, which had been erected in 1707 at a cost of £83, occupied the site of the mediaeval home of the Guild of St Mary and St John the Baptist. It was in a ruinous state, the hall itself more like a barn, and a rather decrepit one at that. Many times the Corporation were urged to replace it, but they had no money to do so, nor apparently any will.

Finally, in 1844, the Conduit Lands Trust took the matter in hand. They voted £2,000 from their funds, " to put the Guildhall to rights once and for all." They practically ejected the Corporation, razed the building to the ground and built the Guildhall which we see today. The cost came to much more than £2,000 in the end— even in those days estimates had a habit of being on the optimistic side.

The architect was the well-known local practitioner, Joseph Potter Jnr. who had started his career, it will be remembered, by sketching the statues on the west front of Wells Cathedral for his father to use in " restoring " the west front at Lichfield with Roman cement. In view of this connection it is perhaps not surprising that he replaced the classical front of the old Guildhall (which matched the architecture of the St Mary's Church of its day) with the Gothic front which it wears today. Inside, a hall with a fine hammerbeam roof and panelled walls provided a meeting place for the Council, a courtroom for the Quarter Sessions and Petty Sessions and a much-improved meeting place for social functions such as county balls. On the floor below prisoners were still confined in dark cells, but alongside them was a new fire-station for the manual pumps which the Conduit Lands Trustees provided for the city. In 1850 the Trustees enrolled a permanent fire brigade of six men to use these pumps. When on duty they were classed as special constables and paid 2/6d (12½ pence) for each fire exercise (the Captain was paid 5/-).

A short distance away from the Guildhall, in Breadmarket Street, is the Guild Church, St Mary's. Although a mediaeval foundation, it has gone through several rebuildings, and in 1850 was a Georgian brick building, covered in stucco. The prevailing enthusiasm for the Gothic brought about a rebuilding of the tower and steeple in that style by G. E. Street in 1853, as a memorial to a former Vicar, Henry Lonsdale, brother of Bishop Lonsdale. It cost £2,410. Street also prepared plans for the rebuilding of the rest of the church, but the money was not forthcoming at the time and so, for the next sixteen years the inhabitants of Lichfield enjoyed the rather unusual spectacle of a rather dowdy stuccoed church in the classical style attached to a splendid grey stone Middle Pointed tower and steeple which could hold its own against the spires of the cathedral.*

In 1868 it was decided to complete the rebuilding of the church as a memorial to Bishop Lonsdale. This time James Fowler of Louth (a Lichfield man by birth) was chosen as architect. To what extent he followed Street's plans is not clear, but the result is a fine example of Victorian Gothic in the Middle Pointed style. The foundation stone was laid by the Earl of Lichfield in April, 1868, and the building completed by April, 1870 at a cost of £8,000. At the time of writing the future of St Mary's Church is in some doubt; it is to be hoped that some fitting use can be found for this fine building which has so many historical associations with the City of Lichfield. For years its appearance has been marred and its interior darkened by the close proximity of the buildings on its south side; what a fine city centre could be achieved by the removal of these and also of the cars which park on the Market Square!

At the east end of St Mary's stood a jumble of old houses. In 1849 these were swept away and replaced by a Corn Exchange and Savings Bank, built at a cost of £2,300 by a local company formed for the purpose. The architects were Thomas Johnson and his son, who by now was in partnership with his father.

A two-storey building in the Tudor style, the bottom storey was built as a market hall or butter-cross, behind an arcade of four-centred arches. This was leased to the City Council on a 999 year lease, for a rent of £25 per annum, and was sub-let to butchers who carried on the tradition of the time when Conduit Street was known as Butchers' Row and contained the city shambles. The Savings Bank was situated in the house at the Bore Street end, and upstairs in the main building were an assembly hall and the actual exchange. Here, under the octagonal lantern, the local farmers and corn merchants met around the customary ring, produced their samples and made their deals. In the adjoining hall concerts were held and lectures given. At one of these, shortly after the Exchange was opened, a talk on the electric telegraph was illustrated by bringing

---

* An illustration of St Mary's in this state appears on the dust cover.

a temporary overhead line from the City Station of the South Staffordshire Railway to the Corn Exchange so that messages could be exchanged with someone in Birmingham. The whole Exchange was purchased by Lichfield Corporation in the year 1900 for a sum of £1,050.

1849 also saw the rebuilding of the schoolroom of the Grammar School in St John Street (now the Council Chamber of Lichfield District Council). Once again Thomas Johnson was the architect; the similarity between this building and the Corn Exchange is easy to see.

By the 1850's the face of Lichfield was changing rapidly. But the greatest change was still to come, and the man who engineered it (literally) was that restless and energetic character, John Robinson McClean. His lease of the South Staffordshire Railway in 1850 was a strategic move of great importance. His first object in getting control of the railway was, as we have seen, to use it as an outlet for the coal mines he was developing on Cannock Chase. But he had another object in mind, too. At that time the towns of the Black Country—Wednesbury, Tipton, Darlaston, Walsall and even Wolverhampton, had a terrible record of diease and epidemics. Large numbers of people crowded together in back-to-back houses, drinking water from wells adjacent to cess-pools, led to terrible outbreaks of cholera. One of the crying needs was for a supply of pure water. McClean noticed that Lichfield had a plentiful supply of this commodity, which came from springs to the west of the city and flowed via the Trunkfield and Leomansley Brooks into the pools which lay across the middle of the city. From Stowe Pool in the west the water ran away through the Curborough Brook to join the River Trent.

Here was a supply of water; eighteen miles away in the Black Country there was a demand for it, and between the two places ran the South Staffordshire Railway. The fertile mind of McClean saw the possibility—waterworks to collect the flow from the streams and springs around Lichfield, a pipeline along the railway into the heart of the Black Country and reservoirs there to store and distribute the water. It appealed to him both as a work of philanthropy and as a business proposition.

LICHFIELD CATHEDRAL, WEST FRONT, 1868
statue of King Charles at top of centre gable. The whole of the West Front is still covered in Roman Cement.

Lichfield Cathedral; Chantrey's " Sleeping Children." Note the Roman cement on the wall bel.
the memorial.

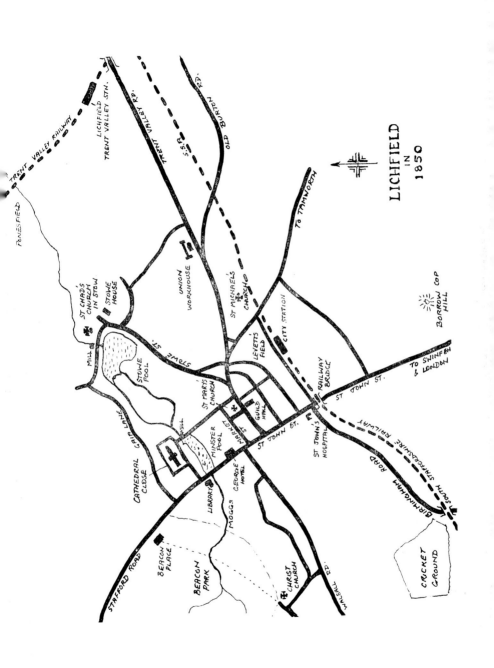

LICHFIELD IN 1850

Lichfield Market Place, c. 1850. Photograph taken on a paper negative.
(Reproduced by permission from the Stone Collection of photographs in Birmingham Reference Library)

TRENT VALLEY STATION LICHFIELD

Seal of the South Staffordshire Railway.
(Reproduced by permission of the National Railway Museum, York.)

SOUTH STAFFORDSHIRE RAILWAY.

ON and after EASTER MONDAY, (April 9th,) this Line will be OPENED for the conveyance of Passengers and Parcels from WALSALL to LICHFIELD, ALREWAS, and BURTON-ON-TRENT, where it joins the Midland, the Leicester and Swannington, and North Staffordshire Railways, and will work in connexion with the trains running on those lines.

Particulars of the times of the departure and arrival of the trains will be shortly advertised.

Walsall Station,   J. D. PAYNE, General Manager.
   March 27th, 1849.

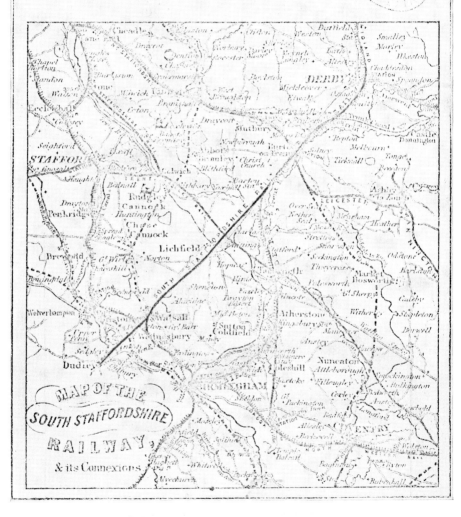

MAP OF THE SOUTH STAFFORDSHIRE RAILWAY, & its Connexions.

THE SOUTH STAFFORDSHIRE RAILWAY.—BRIDGE ACROSS ST. JOHN'S-STREET, LICHFIELD.

FEBRUARY, 1850.

SOUTH STAFFORDSHIRE RAILWAY.

OPENED FROM BIRMINGHAM THROUGH WALSALL & LICHFIELD TO BURTON

Where it joins the Leicester and Swannington, North Staffordshire and Midland Railways; by which a great saving of mileage in Railway Communication will be gained between the South Staffordshire district and Derby, Sheffield, and the North. London Time will be observed at all Stations.

UP TRAINS.

Miles from Burton.	STATIONS.	WEEK DAYS. 1 & 2 Class.	Parly 1 & 3 Class.	1 & 2 Class.	Goods. Parly 1 2 & 3.	SUNDAYS. 1 2 & 3 Class.	1 & 2 Class.	1 2 & 3 Class.
	LEAVE	a. m.	a. m.	p. m.	p. m.	a. m.	p. m.	p. m.
—	DERBY	8 0	11 15	4 0	6 30	—	—	—
—	LEICESTER	7 0	10 20	2 45	5 30	—	—	—
—	UTTOXETER...	7 30	9 35	1 5	4 40	—	—	—
—	RUGELEY	8 38	12 24	4 29	—	—	—	—
—	**BURTON**	8 45	12 15	4 45	7 30	—	—	—
4	BARTON & WALTON ...	8 55	12 26	4 55	7 42	—	—	—
7¼	**ALREWAS**	9 5	12 37	5 2	7 48	—	—	—
11½	TRENT VALLEY JUNCTION	9 15	12 49	5 12	—	—	—	—
Trent Valley.	RUGELEY Arrival at ...	9 41	3 45	7 45	—	—	—	—
	STAFFORD Arrival at	10 5	2 12	8 20	—	—	—	—
12½	**LICHFIELD**	9 20	12 55	5 18	8 10	9 40	3 15	9 10
15¾	HAMMERWICH ...	—	1 5	—	8 20	9 47	—	9 18
18	BROWNHILLS	9 32	1 12	5 31	8 30	9 52	3 28	9 23
20	**PELSALL**	9 37	1 18	5 36	8 36	9 56	3 38	9 27
21¼	RUSHALL	—	1 22	—	8 40	10 0	—	9 30
23	**WALSALL** ...	9 45	1 30	5 45	8 50	10 5	3 45	9 35
26¼	NEWTON ROAD	—	1 36	5 51	8 58	10 15	3 53	9 45
29¾	PERRY BARR... ...	9 57	1 42	5 58	9 6	10 21	4 0	9 51
33¼	Arrive at **BIRMINGHAM** ...	10 15	2 0	6 15	9 20	10 30	4 15	10 0
	Leave for				a. m.	p. m.		a. m.
—	LONDON...	10 30	4 0	8 8	12 15	12 30	—	12 15
—	GLOUCESTER	11 0	2 30	6 30	1 40	—	5 0	1 43

DOWN TRAINS.

Miles from Birm'm.	STATIONS.	WEEK DAYS. Parly 1 2 & 3 Class.	1 & 2 Class.	1 & 2 Class.	Goods. Parly 1 2 & 3	SUNDAYS. 1 2 & 3 Class.	1 & 2 Class.	1 2 & 3 Class.
	LEAVE	a. m.	a. m. 7 15	noon.	p. m.	a. m.	a. m.	p. m.
—	LONDON	—	9 0	12 0	5 0	—	10 0	—
—	GLOUCESTER	7 0	9 38	12 35	5 5	—	—	—
			p. m.	p. m.			p. m.	
—	**BIRMINGHAM** ...	10 5	1 15	4 45	8 45	8 30	2 0	8 0
3½	PERRY BARR	10 12	1 23	4 53	8 53	8 35	2 8	8 8
7	NEWTON ROAD	10 20	1 32	5 2	9 0	8 46	2 16	8 16
10¼	**WALSALL**... ...	10 30	1 45	5 10	9 20	8 55	2 25	8 25
12	RUSHALL	10 35	—	—	9 25	9 0	—	8 30
13¼	**PELSALL**	10 39	1 55	5 19	9 30	9 3	2 35	8 33
15¼	BROWNHILLS	10 45	2 0	5 25	9 35	9 9	2 39	8 39
17½	HAMMERWICH	10 50	—	*	9 40	9 14	—	8 44
20¾	**LICHFIELD**	11 0	2 15	5 40	9 50	9 23	2 53	8 53
21¾	TRENT VALLEY JUNCTION	11 4	2 20	5 45	—	—	—	—
Trent Valley.	STAFFORD Departure from	8 20	12 0	3 53	—	—	—	—
	RUGELEY Departure from	8 38	12 24	4 29	—	—	—	—
26	**ALREWAS**	11 15	2 29	5 54	10 5	—	—	—
29¼	BARTON & WALTON ...	11 22	—	6 0	10 10	—	—	—
33¼	Arrive at **LURTON**	11 35	2 45	6 15	10 30	—	—	—
—	RUGELEY	—	3 45	7 45	—	—	—	—
—	UTTOXETER...	12 25	4 40	7 15	—	—	—	—
—	LEICESTER	1 50	6 10	—	—	—	—	—
—	DERBY	12 15	3 30	8 45	1 55	—	—	—

* Calls at Hammerwich on Tuesdays.

FARES.

DAY TICKETS

BETWEEN

Birmingham and Walsall,

First Class, **2s. 6d.** Second Class, **1s. 8d.**

Birmingham and Lichfield,

First Class, **4s.** Second Class, **3s.**

Walsall and Lichfield,

First Class, **3s.** Second Class, **2s.**

CHILDREN under three years of age FREE; above three and under twelve years of age HALF-PRICE.

PASSENGERS LUGGAGE.—The Company do not hold themselves responsible for Luggage unless booked and paid for according to its value. 100lbs. weight of Luggage allowed to First and Second Class and 56lbs. to Third Class Passengers, *not being merchandise or other articles carried for hire or profit*; any excess of that weight will be charged one farthing per lb.

DAY TICKETS (not transferable) are issued from all Stations.

WOLVERHAMPTON.

OMNIBUSES leave the Red Cow Coach Office, WOLVERHAMPTON, at 9 15 and 11 45 a.m., 4 0 and 6 35 p.m. to meet the 10 30 a.m., 1 45, 5 10, and 9 20 p.m. Down Trains, and the 1 20, and 8 50 p.m. Up Trains at WALSALL, returning in connection with the 9 45 a.m., 1 30, 5 45, and 8 50 p.m. Up Trains, and the 5 10 p.m. Down Train.

McCLEAN & STILEMAN, ENGINEERS. HORATIO BARNETT, SECRETARY. J. D. PAYNE, GENERAL MANAGER.

J. R. ROBINSON, ALBION PRINTING OFFICE, DIGBETH, WALSALL.

South West View of the Union Workhouse at Lichfield.

(J. Buckler, 1843.)

Bank note of Palmer and Green's Bank, Lichfield. Note Mr Lawton's signature in bottom left corner.

Cheque of Palmer and Greene's Bank, Lichfield.

*Proposed clock tower over the statue of Dr. Johnson in Lichfield Market
Place, 1856.*

PATIENCE SWINFEN
Portrait by Samuel West. c. 1850
(Reproduced by permission from the Stone Collection of photographs in Birmingham Reference Library)

Swinfen Hall (Front) 1900
(Reproduced by permission from the Stone Collection of photographs in Birmingham Reference Library)

Swinfen Hall (Rear) 1900
(Reproduced by permission from the Stone Collection of photographs in Birmingham Reference Library)

Victorian Bower—Collecting for the Lifeboat.
(Reproduced by permission from the Stone Collection of photographs in Birmingham Reference Library)

Victorian Bower Day. Civic Party outside the Guildhall.
Note the Town Crier with top hat and staff.
(Reproduced by permission from the Stone Collection of photographs in Birmingham Reference Library)

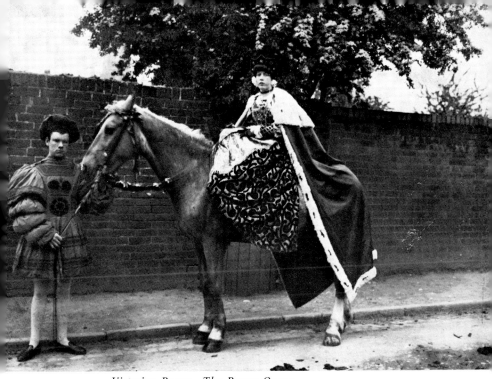

Victorian Bower—The Bower Queen.
roduced by permission from the Stone Collection of photographs in Birmingham Reference Library)

Victorian Bower—Distributing the Bower Cakes.
roduced by permission from the Stone Collection of photographs in Birmingham Reference Library)

Victorian Bower—Holloway's Travelling Theatre.
(Reproduced by permission from the Stone Collection of photographs in Birmingham Reference Library)

This Room Is Equipped With

Edison Electric Light.

Do not attempt to light with match. Simply turn key on wall by the door.

The use of Electricity for lighting is in no way harmful
to health, nor does it affect the soundness of sleep.

By 1895 several houses in Lichfield had electric light. With every installation a number of copies of this notice was supplied for the uninitiated.

F. M. & J. WAIT,

CABINET MAKERS, UPHOLSTERERS,

UNDERTAKERS, &c.,

25, Bird Street, Lichfield.

FUNERALS FURNISHED AT ANY DISTANCE.

Oak, Elm, and the Patent Metallic Coffins and Shells supplied on the shortest notice.

—·o—

BEDDING AND MATTRESSES CLEANED AND RE-MADE.

—o—

CHURCH FURNISHING—

Matting, Kneels, Hassocks, Seating, supplied or Re-covered.

Two Victorian Businesses that are still with us.

J. SALLOWAY,

(Successor to, and upwards of 25 years with the late Mr. C. Thorneloe*);*

Watch, Clock, & Jewellery Manufacturer,

(NEARLY OPPOSITE THE POST OFFICE),

BORE STREET, LICHFIELD.

Clocks and Watches with latest improvements, perfect for time, beauty, and workmanship.

Presentation Bronze and Marble Time-Pieces, Artistic Jewellery, Gold and Silver Medals for Cyclists, Cricketers, and all other Athletic Sports, Real Whitby Jet Ornaments, Accurate Barometers and Thermometers. All kinds of Clocks, Jewellery, Musical Boxes, etc., repaired on the premises at moderate charges.

CLOCKS IN THE COUNTRY ATTENDED TO.

...nel Forster, Joint Master, South Staffordshire Hunt. Here seen in his capacity of High Sheriff of Herefordshire, about to leave home for an official function.

Manley Hall—at the opening they danced all night.

LT.-COLONEL M. A. W. SWINFEN-BROUN
Commanding 3rd Battalion, South Staffordshire Regiment (Militia) c. 1895

Lysways Hall, Near Lichfield, c. 1890
Home of the South Staffordshire Hunt. Sir Charles Forster (left) and Colonel Villiers Forster (rig
Joint Masters.

He set to work to float a company (a peculiarly appropriate phrase in this case!). Following the example of the railway, it was to be known as the South Staffordshire Waterworks Company, and McClean's friend Richard Chawner was to be its first Chairman. The Board of Directors included two other of his business associates of the railway days, Mr C. S. Forster and Captain Dyott of Freeford and many of the leading property owners of the district, including Lord Ward of Himley Hall, later Earl of Dudley. Mr Wainwright, then Mayor of Dudley, took a great interest in the scheme and acted as the Company solicitor in the Black Country district. Dyott & Sons were the solicitors at the Lichfield end, carrying out all the complicated negotiations with the Corporation. The engineers to the company were, of course, McClean and Stileman.

The first scheme, produced in 1851, was for a reservoir at Lichfield, in the Friary in the area which is now the Clock Tower gardens; this would be fed by the Leomansley Brook. Water from the reservoir would be pumped by steam engines in a pumping station at Sandfields, along the railway to Walsall.

McClean had reckoned on a daily minimum supply of four million gallons from the Lichfield stream, but in this he was over-optimistic and his scheme had to be modified and extended. As eventually embodied in the Act of Parliament it consisted of a reservoir at Hanch Hall, to the north of Lichfield, collecting water from the Seedy Mill Brook which was then brought to Sandfields by a tunnel running through the middle of Lichfield. In addition, a reservoir at Ponesfield was to collect the flow of Leomansley Brook.

The South Staffordshire Waterworks Act received the Royal assent on 4th August, 1853. By its terms the Company was authorised to supply water to Lichfield, Walsall, Wednesbury, Darlaston, Bilston, Willenhall, West Bromwich, Rowley Regis, Sedgley, Tipton, Dudley and Oldbury. For its supply the Company was authorised to take the water of certain springs and streams which rise at the base of a wide sweep of hills to the west of Lichfield, to collect it in large reservoirs near the city and to force it by engine-power through a large pipe to be laid along the side of the South Staffordshire Railway, to reservoirs to be constructed at Walsall, Wednesbury and Dudley Port, from which points it could be piped all over the district. The capital of the Company was fixed at £160,000 in £10 shares, with additional borrowing powers up to £30,000. Each shareholder was to have one vote for every share up to fifty, then one for every five shares up to one hundred and after that one for every ten shares. The minimum qualification for directors was fifty shares.

In its early stages the project faced many difficulties and setbacks, but it was typical of McClean, the originator of the scheme, that his faith in the ultimate success of the undertaking never wavered and he had so far the courage of his convictions that on two separate occasions, both before and after they had commenced operations, he offered to take over the entire concern on lease and pay the shareholders a fixed dividend of five per cent.

CHAPTER VI

The Lichfield Pools

In the year 1840 Dr. W. Rawson, a medical practitioner in Lichfield, published a pamphlet entitled " An Inquiry into the History and Influence of the Lichfield Water, Intended to show the Necessity of an Immediate and Final Drainage of the Pools."*

The title itself leaves us in no doubt as to Dr Rawson's feelings about the pools, and his theme was the bad effect they had on the health of Lichfield people. He began his pamphlet with a brief historical survey in which he showed that in the year 1300 there were three pools—the Upper Pool, which covered the low-lying ground to the north of the Friary (the area now known as the Festival Gardens, laid out to commemorate the Festival of Britain in 1951); the Middle Pool which lay to the south and south-west of the Cathedral in the area now occupied by Minster Pool and the Museum Gardens; and Stow Pool which still exists today (with an e added to its name). In 1310 Bishop Langton divided the Middle Pool into two by building a causeway across it. The water to the west of the causeway became the Bishop's Pool and that to the east became Minster Pool. A mill was built at the outflow of Minster Pool, and another one at the outflow of Stow Pool. Both these belonged to the Bishop as the Lord of the Manor, but in the Reign of Elizabeth I the Lordship of the Manor, together with the ownership of the Pools and the Mills, passed to the Corporation of Lichfield. The Senior Baliff (now the Mayor) has been the Lord of the Manor ever since.

---

* Lomax, Lichfield, 1840.

The pools are fed by two streams rising in the west of the city, Leomansley Brook and Sandford Brook (sometimes known as Trunkfield Brook). As these are not very fast-running there has always been a tendency for the pools to silt up, and as there was a natural tendency for the townspeople to use them as a sewer and for various trades such as tanners to establish themselves on the margin, the unpleasant and malodorous condition of the waters can well be imagined. The occupiers of the two mills, under the conditions of their leases, were supposed to keep the pools clean, but it was an impossible task.

By 1730 the Bishop's Pool, on the west side of the causeway, had silted up completely and was a swamp crossed by gutters, cuts and ditches. It became known as the Swan Moggs.* Much the same had happened to Stow Pool, which had dwindled from 22 acres to a mere 7 acres by St Chad's Church, leaving a large area of moggs bounded by two streams. Only Minster Pool retained its form as a sheet of water, and in 1773 it was extensively cleaned and laid out in serpentine form by public subscription at the instigation of Anna Seward. From then on efforts were made to keep it clean as an amenity of the city, but by the time Dr Rawson published his pamphlet in 1840 the cost of scouring Minster Pool had risen to £600, and the main sewer from the Close still emptied into it, although the town had by this time been supplied with an underground system which deposited its sewage in the Curborough Brook beyond Pones Mill.

It is understandable, therefore why Dr Rawson considered the pools so injurious to the health of Lichfield's inhabitants considering them to be responsible for the " low fever " which he maintained was particularly prevalent in the town. He also drew attention to the frequent fogs due to the waters, and the consequent incidence of respiratory diseases. As an example of this he writes, " On Sunday the 11th of November, 1838, a chilling, dense and particularly damp fog was experienced in Lichfield immediately before and about noon. At which precisely same date the suburbs

---

* The term "moggs" for a bog or swamp is peculiar to Lichfield. According to Dr Rawson, it was derived from a family called Mogys who owned the Swan Moggs at one time.

of the town presented only a comparative haziness of the atmosphere, while on Whittington Heath the air was clear, the sun as bright and the sky as blue as they could be expected in a frosty November! Viewed, however, from the summit of the Heath the site of Lichfield appeared—literally speaking—as if palled in the gloom of night, a clear blue sky surmounting the circumscribed darkness."

These circumstances are not unknown today, though fortunately we now only suffer from fogs, and not the " smogs " of Dr Rawson's days, caused by the hundreds of chimneys belching out smoke and producing the " gloom of night."

The doctor's remedy was a drastic one—nothing less than the filling in of the pools—and he concluded by saying, " The Lichfield Pools, without vast human effort, must rapidly disappear by the rigid operation of natural laws."

Little did he imagine, when he wrote those words, that the vast human effort he visualised would come to pass before long. It came, of course, as a result of John Robinson McClean's idea of tapping the Lichfield waters to supply the Black Country. His first scheme, proposed in 1851, would have diverted the streams into a new reservoir by the Friary—the old Upper Pool in fact—and with their supply cut off Minster Pool and Stowe Pool would have dried up and the mills at Dam Street, Stowe and Pones Mill would have ground to a halt. No doubt this would have delighted the heart of Dr Rawson, but the Corporation and townsfolk were not amused. Smelly though they might be, the pools were a part at Lichfield, hallowed by time, and the citizens were not going to part with them. The scheme was dropped, and when the South Staffordshire Waterworks Company received their Act of Incorporation in 1853, the plans put forward in the Act made provision for the retention of the pools. Minster Pool was to be cleaned out, Stow Pool to be cleaned and the water level raised by means of an embankment, thus restoring the sheet of water to its original 22 acres. On top of the embankment, at the request of Lichfield Corporation, was to be a " promenade." In addition to this a new reservoir was to be constructed at Pones Mill, in the area now known as The Millpond. From here water was to be pumped in 30 inch diameter iron pipes along the London North Western Railway's track to Streethay, and from there along the track of the South Staffordshire Railway to the City Station. Here the pipe turned left and ran alongside St John Street to a small circular reservoir near Barrow Cop hill, on the site of what is now the playing field of King Edward VI School. Water would be stored in the reservoir and descend by gravity as required to the railway track again, and then along the track to Sandfields and into a pumping shaft, 90 feet deep, below the engines which were to pump it to Walsall along the length of the railway track.

In addition to this scheme there was to be a second one, which involved constructing yet another reservoir at Seedy Mill, near Elmhurst, to the north of the city. This would collect water from the Bilston and Bourne Brooks which rose on Cannock Chase, and from the reservoir the water would be conveyed by a tunnel which would empty into Stow Pool near the Parchment Cottages. This would have involved quite a considerable feat of engineering for although the level of Stow Pool was only ten feet below that of the proposed reservoir at Seedy Mill, quite a high ridge of ground intervened so that at one place the tunnel would be 80 feet below the surface.

Work began in December, 1855 on the sinking of the shaft at Sandfields, and also on the cleaning out of Minster Pool, after diverting the stream which ran into it. Five feet of mud was removed from the bottom of the pool and in the process many interesting relics were discovered including cannon balls and mortar shells from the Civil War.* Beneath the mud they found a strata of red and white sandstone which led engineers to suggest that Minster Pool had been formed originally by the quarrying of stone for the building of the cathedral (not the present one, but the Saxon or Norman building).

The mud was disposed of by offering it to local farmers to take away to put on their fields, so for the next few months the inhabitants of Lichfield had to put up with discomfort of farm carts passing through their streets dripping and oozing slime everywhere.

---

* Now in Lichfield Museum (closed).

The official opening of the works took place in February when the first sod was turned by Lord Ward of Himley, a Director of the South Staffordshire Waterworks Company. A special train was laid on by Mr McClean at his own expense to bring Lord Ward and a large number of gentlemen from Dudley, Tipton, Wednesbury and Walsall. They were met at Lichfield station by the Earl of Lichfield and the city's two M.P's, Lord Waterpark and Lord Alfred Paget. A procession was formed and moved off to Stow Pool, being joined at the Guildhall by the Deputy Mayor, W. H. Hewitt Esq., the Corporation and the Town Clerk, Charles Simpson Esq., and Lord Hatherton, the Lord Lieutenant of Staffordshire.

The spot chosen for the ceremony was in the fields at the western end of the pool, where the embankment was to be raised. Unfortunately the conveyance of the land to the company had not been completed in time for the ceremony, and Mr Dyott, the company's solicitor, had to pay Mr Rogers, the owner of the land, the sum of £4 for the use of it.

A platform had been erected for the convenience of the guests, and a spade and barrow were in readiness. The spade, made by Mr Linden of Birmingham, was of silver, in the shape of a shield, highly polished and inscribed:—

" This spade was used by the Rt. Hon. Lord Ward in turning the first sod of the South Staffordshire Waterworks Company at Iichfield on 22nd February, 1856.

Chairman: Richard Croft Chawner Esq., The Abnalls, Lichfield.

Directors: Samuel Holden, Dudley.
Edwards Bagnall Dimmock, Wolverhampton.
Richard Smith, Dudley.
Samuel Mills, Darlaston.
Richard Jesson, Walsall.
Sampson Lloyd, Wednesbury.
Thomas Walker, Wednesbury.
Hervy Wyatt, Stafford.

Engineers: Messers McClean & Stileman and Henry Martin."

The handle of the spade was of polished mahogany, and the wheelbarrow,* made by Mr Elliot, builder of Wolverhampton, was also of mahogany.

Receiving the spade, Lord Ward loosened a large sod which he then placed in the barrow and wheeled to the other end of the platform, amid the applause of the assembled multitude. Advancing to the front of the platform, Lord Ward then said : —

" Gentlemen of Staffordshire, and inhabitants of the district generally; I cannot help thinking that this is a great day in the annals of Lichfield—a great day because the work we are met to inaugurate is calculated to administer to one of the most essential of all wants in the course of everyday existence—the supply of water (hear, hear)—and most gratifying it is that you, in this town, are not only abundantly and purely supplied yourselves, but that from the large and copious supply you can extend to a district so wanting in it—the mining district of South Staffs—a large and never-failing quantity of pure water, without in any way trenching on your own requirements. You who enjoy it, to whose houses it is brought in any quantity at all hours, know not what it is to live in a district where it is not to be had by night at all, and during the day only at great expense . . . In these days all those who have anything like leisure, all those who have the means at their disposal, are, more than ever has been the case in England's history. disposed to turn their attention to the well-being of the community at large (hear, hear)—but be assured as great as . . ."

At this point the platform collapsed from the weight of the immense crowd upon it, but as it was only raised a foot from the ground, no one was hurt.

Lord Ward remarked jocularly, " There's one comfort about this, we're at the bottom of it," and continued his speech wishing success to the undertaking.

---

* The wheelbarrow can be seen today in the South Staffordshire Waterworks Co's museum at Brindley Bank, Rugeley.

Richard Chawner, the Company chairman, then addressed the assembly, expressing the hope that in disturbing that stagnant pool (laughter) they should benefit not only the mining districts, but also the City of Lichfield.

The procession then reformed and proceeded via Stow Pool into the city with flying colours,* through streets lined with people, to the George Hotel, where 130 sat down to dinner. The special train returned to Dudley at 7.30.

In view of Lord Ward's congratulatory remarks to the inhabitants of Lichfield about their abundant water supply, it was ironic that only a few weeks later that selfsame supply would begin to fail. The cause was the deep shaft that the waterworks company was sinking at Sandfields. For centuries Lichfield had been supplied with water piped into the city by that fine old Lichfield institution, the Conduit Lands Trust, from springs at Aldershaw, to the south of the city. The new shaft which was being sunk at Sandfields was close to these and began to fill with water as it went lower. Pumps had to be employed to get rid of this water, and as a result the surrounding water table fell and the Conduit Lands springs began to fail. Among the inhabitants of Lichfield, many people put this down to the draining of the pools, as did the writer of the following letter:

" To the Editor,

The Staffordshire Advertiser,

Sir,

I just drop your readers a line of information to announce the glorious position of this city and the suburbs thereof, without water this day! We have at last reached the climax when grumbling, either in Latin or English would be both a duty and a necessity; for the doctor and the druggist are unable to retail the pure aqua to the invalids under their care; the milkwoman cannot mingle from the pump two parts to one, and even the washerwoman and the

---

* Probably the ward standards which were carried in the Bower Procession and on other special occasions such as this.

brewer ought to begin trembling in anticipation of the failure of their occupations, in consequence of the draining of the pools. Surely the water is not ' locked up ' in the bank, even if the funds there are,* but as to the Feoffees† and the Waterworks, they appear to want winding up, like Paddy's watch.

Yours etc.

' Caustic ' "

(*Staffordshire Advertiser* 18/2/56).

Presumably the supply of water was resumed, as no more complaints appear, but the patience of Lichfield people was becoming a little strained. Worse was to come however, for as 1856 drew to a close the waterworks company announced that they proposed to apply for another Act, the South Staffordshire Waterworks Amendment Act of 1857 as it eventually became. Under the terms of this Act, the idea of a reservoir at Pones Mill was abandoned, together with the aqueduct along the railway lines and the reservoir at Barrow Cop. Instead, Stow Pool was to be enlarged for use as the main reservoir and the two streams that supplied it would be put underground in brick tunnel where they ran through the city. Another brick-lined tunnel would take water out of Stow Pool in the opposite direction, under Dam Street and Bird Street, across Beacon Park to Townsfields; from there across towards the Bowling Green Inn and so on to the pumping shaft at Sandfields which it would enter at a depth of 68 feet. The reservoir at Seedy Mill and the tunnel from there to Stow Pool was to remain part of the plan. Powers were to be requested for the compulsory purchase of the mills at Seedy Mill, Leomansley Mill (a worsted spinning mill), the Union Mill in Dam Street and Stow Mill by St Chad's Church.

But the clause in the Bill that caused the most consternation was the one which would have given the South Staffordshire Waterworks Company the right to fill in Minster Pool " and turn it into a place of recreation."

---

* This reference is to the failure of the Lichfield Bank which took place about this time. (See Chapter VII).
† Feoffees—the Trustees of the Conduit Lands Trust.

The very idea that this historic piece of water should be done away with, and a feature of Lichfield which had existed for centuries be lost was too much for the citizens. They were up in arms at once, and the Mayor was petitioned to call a public meeting to discuss the matter. The meeting took place on 15th December, 1856 in a packed Guildhall. Richard Chawner was there as Chairman of the Waterworks Company to explain the plan to the meeting. It was undesirable, he said, to have an open area of water which was used for a domestic supply, in the middle of a city. People might throw dead dogs and other unpleasant objects into it. But his words went unheeded. The only one to support him was Dr Rawson. Mr Chawner went on to say that the company had set aside the sum of £500 with which they would lay out the site of Minster Pool as public gardens. They would even provide an ornamental fountain in the middle of the gardens and a supply of water to go with it! But the citizens of Lichfield were not to be won over with such blandishments. They voted unanimously to keep the Minster Pool and the Waterworks Company had to give in. The matter which finally settled it was was the attitude of the Dean and Chapter. Up till that time the sewer from the Close had emptied into Minster Pool, and whatever scheme was adopted for the waterworks it would require a new sewer to be made to serve the Close. Now the Dean and Chapter announced that if the Minster Pool were to be filled in, they would not agree to the Close being connected to the new sewer. In this case, presumably, it would have gone on using the old system with its sewage discharging into the new public gardens!

The plans were therefore amended to retain Minster Pool as a sheet of water and the proposed brick tunnels were abandoned. Instead a thirty-inch cast-iron pipe, supported on brick piers, was laid along the bed of the pool, extending under Dam Street and the adjacent meadows and into Stow Pool. This pipe would carry water from the Leomansley and Trunkfield Brooks through the area which is now the Muscum Gardens, under Bird Street, through the Minster Pool below the surface of the water and into Stow Pool. It could also be used to convey water in the opposite direction, *out* of Stow Pool back into Museum Gardens where it would be diverted into another pipe leading it to a large well-shaft in the vicinity of the present tennis courts. From this well-shaft a tunnel led, via another eight shafts, to the pumping shaft at Sandfields.

While water was being carried in this direction, the outflow of the two brooks would be turned into Minster Pool, from where it would overflow into Stow Pool by yet another pipe. This was the system which now proposed and which in due course was carried out. It is still being used today, though water is no longer drawn from Stowe Pool (to give it its modern spelling) by the South Staffordshire Waterworks Company.

The scheme for a reservoir at Seedy Mill was retained, together with the tunnel to Stow Pool, though this was to form a later phase.

In this form the new Act was duly obtained and the work of construction proceeded. The soil from the tunnel and the eight well-shafts along its route was deposited on the Swan Moggs, filling in that ancient swamp and removing one of Lichfield's oldest health-hazards. When this had been completed the area was laid out as a public garden, on the lines which had been proposed for Minster Pool. Trees were planted, flowerbeds laid out, and that Victorian essential to any public park, a bandstand, was provided. So came into being the Museum Gardens, one of Lichfield's pleasantest amenities, and the cause of much civic pride in its time. It even acquired its fountain in due course, presented by the Rev. Chancellor Law in 1871. Its inauguration was the excuse for another civic occasion, with a large concourse of people, the usual speeches and the band of the Staffordshire Militia to play Handel's Water Music as Chancellor Law turned on the fountain. It produced a six foot spray and used 150 gallons an hour, which led to some complaints at times of water shortage.

While Stow Pool, the tunnel and the tunnel shafts were in course of construction, another contractor was busy laying the cast-iron pipes along the railway line to Walsall. They had been manufactured by Messers Cochram of Woodside Ironworks near Dudley (on the line, be it noted of Mr McClean's South Staffordshire Railway).

At Sandfields, over the large pumping shaft, an engine house was erected to contain the pumping engines. These were supplied by the famous Birmingham firm of James Watt & Co., formerly Boulton & Watt, and they have an interesting history. They were not new, having been constructed in 1846 for the South Devon Atmospheric Railway. The atmospheric railway system was one of the many ingenious inventions of that time which failed because though excellent in theory, they were in advance of the technology of the time. The idea was to dispense with locomotives and instead have stationary engines at intervals of three miles along the line to provide the power. This was transmitted to the train by means of a circular tube, usually 15 inches in diameter, and made of cast iron, which was laid between the rails. The tube had a slot along the top and the front coach of a train had an arm projecting downwards from underneath it. This arm passed through the slot in the top of the tube and was connected to a piston inside. The method of operation was to exhaust the air from the tube in front of the piston by means of air-pumps situated at each engine house. This would produce a vacuum in front of the piston which would suck it along the tube. Only one more thing was necessary, and this was some method which would seal the slot in the tube in front of the piston, but would open as the piston arm passed. The method employed was a continuous flap or valve of leather, and this was the weak point of the system, for although it worked well at first, enabling speeds of up to seventy miles an hour to be achieved, the leather soon perished or was eaten by rats and it would not function. This was what occured on the South Devon Railway. When the railway, between Exeter and Newton Abbot, was being built the Engineer, Isambard Brunel, persuaded the company to adopt the atmospheric system, and the first section of the line, between Exeter and Teignmouth, was opened and operated by atmospheric power. However, the faults mentioned above caused the directors to have second thoughts and they abandoned the atmospheric principle before completing the line. In consequence a number of stationary engines and air-pumps which they had ordered were left on the hands of the manufacturers, James Watt. After a lapse of ten years four of them were being disposed of to the South Staffordshire Waterworks Company.

They were installed at the Sandfields Pumping Station and for the next sixty-five years they served their new owners well, pumping water from the great pit beneath them along the railway line to Walsall. They were removed in 1924 and a plaque giving their history placed on the wall of the engine house. It is still there today, though the engine house itself has changed. They were beam engines, each of some 85 working horse-power, pumping 1,144,368 gallons per day.

The first phase of the construction of the waterworks was completed in 1858 and water began to flow along the pipe to Walsall on the 26th of October.

For the second phase, the Seedy Mill scheme, a new Act had to be obtained, the South Staffordshire Waterworks Amendment Act of 1864. The original idea of a tunnel to Stow Pool was abandoned and instead it was proposed to bring it down Grange Lane, through Wheel Lane into Beacon Street and then along Beacon Street until it reached a point just before the entrance to the Cathedral Close. Here the tunnel turned right to cross Beacon Park and join the tunnel from Stow Pool to Sandfields. In due course this scheme was carried out. Along the length of the tunnel no less than twenty-six well-shafts were sunk to collect additional water, all connected to each other by the tunnel. The top of one of these shafts can be seen in the car park of the Angel Croft Hotel; an enclosure about twelve feet square surrounded by cast-iron railings. The upheaval caused by this work to those living in the north of the city must have been considerable.

At Sandfields a new pumping shaft had to be constructed to deal with the additional water. Over it was constructed a second engine house containing a single Cornish beam engine, constructed by an Oldbury firm, Jonas & George Davies. This Victorian monster (it extends upward through three storeys of the engine house) is still in existence at the time of writing, though it has not been steamed for many years. Too large to be removed without demolishing the engine house which contains it, it remains as a monument to an industrial age now long gone.

The whole of the Lichfield waterworks scheme was not completed until 1873, and ever since it has carried on its function of supplying pure water to the " Black Country " and to an ever-increasing area of South Staffordshire. In 1968, as Minster and Stowe Pools were no longer required as reservoirs, they were handed back to their original owners the Mayor and Corporation of Lichfield and now form two of the most important public amenities in the city.

The building of the waterworks produced one of the greatest changes in the face of Lichfield throughout the whole of the 19th Century. It was not a change that was universally approved. Though Mr Chawner might see Stowe mere as " a stagnant pool," it appeared differently to other eyes. The Reverend John Graham, who came to Lichfield as Rector of St Chad's in 1853, gave the following idyllic description of it.

" On the west of the ancient church there was a natural lake, with the waters rippling pleasantly on the pebbly shore. An old mill, turned by water from the stream, stood picturesquely on the sloping bank; a waterfall over the natural rock carried the overflow of the lake down towards the meadows under a sloping, grassy, hillocky piece of ground, covered in springtime with primroses and violets nestling in mossy coves. Here the lady-birch hung her long tresses over the lapsing stream, and the ashes, towering elms and stately oaks reared their heads heavenwards. Now, alas, all that has passed away. The requirements of modern civilisation and sanitary needs have completely changed the aspect of the scene. The waters of the lake have been utilized for public wants by the South Staffordshire Waterworks Company, the mill is gone, and the rushing stream and the rocky pools have been filled in and levelled."

CHAPTER VII

Lichfield in 1856

The year 1856 was an extraordinary one in the annals of Lichfield. It was the sort of year that newspaper editors dream of, with one momentous happening following another in rapid succession. Right through the year there was the upheaval caused by the building of the waterworks, with the attendant alarms and excursions, petitions to the Mayor and letters to the papers. It was also the year when Sir Gilbert Scott began his work at the Cathedral, though at the time it is doubtful if many people in Lichfield realised the full significance of what he was starting to do.

But apart from these happenings there were " human " stories enough to keep the newspaper reporters busy day and night and the tongues of Lichfield people wagging all the time.

From neighbouring Rugeley came the horrid story of Palmer the Poisoner—a case of multiple murder that achieved national interest and eventually became part of criminal history. After his trial at the Old Bailey, reported in great detail, and his subsequent conviction, he was brought back to Stafford for execution. At this time hanging was still carried out in public, and it was estimated that some 30,000 people turned up to witness the spectacle outside Stafford Gaol. A special train ran from Lichfield and from all the other stations for miles around Stafford, and for those who could not attend the papers gave full details of Palmer's last moments.

The execution took place outside the main entrance to Stafford Gaol, where the scaffold had been erected. Barriers had been placed across streets leading to the gaol so that the number of people entering the area could be regulated. Women were not admitted through the barriers, but several watched from the

windows of nearby houses, one, according to a newspaper report
" with the aid of a glass, through which she coolly watched the
proceedings."

The execution was fixed for eight a.m., and all through the
night people were arriving and taking up their positions. Ladders
were arranged against the walls of the gaol so that any who fainted
at the front of the crowd could be rescued by this means. All night
trains kept arriving at Stafford bringing spectators, and all night
the roads leading to the town were thronged with people on foot,
on horse or in conveyances. But on the whole, reported the papers,
they were a sober crowd and the " sporting gentlemen " who in
times past had come to witness hangings after carousing together
all night were entirely absent. The public houses were open all
night, but so too were the Methodist Chapels, where the public
were invited to join in prayers for the condemned man.

There was a drizzle of rain all night, but it stopped just before
eight o'clock. A minute before eight the prison bell began to toll,
and the crowd knew that the procession had started from the
condemned cell. The cry went around the crowd, " Hats off " and
then a hush fell as the gates opened and the procession, led by the
High Sheriff, emerged. Palmer, though deathly pale walked with
a firm step to the drop. The executioner, a drover named Smith
who was dressed in a white smock-frock, shook hands with him,
pinioned his hands and adjusted the hood and noose, and a second
later the drop fell.

Most of the crowd remained while the condemned man's body
hung for the statutory hour. After watching its removal they
dispersed.

On the same day, at Lichfield, the City Council met and fixed
the rate for the coming year at threepence in the pound.

The year had opened with a shock for many citizens and for
most of the businesses and institutions in Lichfield, with the failure
of the city's principal bank, Messers Palmer & Greene.

At this time the large joint stock banks were still in their infancy, and throughout the provinces most of the banking was carried out by local businesses, usually partnerships. These local banks all issued their own bank-notes, which in theory were backed by gold—in other words, anyone holding a bank-note could take it to the bank at any time and exchange it for gold sovereigns which were then legal tender. But there was a constant temptation, of course, for banks to stretch their credit by issuing more bank-notes than they had gold to back them with. Even where this did not apply, bankers in the provinces tended to deposit as much of their gold as they could with London bankers or the Bank of England where it would earn them interest. Consequently there was always a fear of a " run on the bank." If word got around that all was not well, customers would flock to the bank to change their notes into gold, and queues would form in the street outside. A member of the bank staff would have to be despatched hastily in a post-chaise to London to draw on the gold reserves, while back at the bank every possible ruse would be employed to slow up business until the gold would arrive. But in cases where there were more notes than gold the bank could not meet its commitments and the result was failure of the bank and bankruptcy for its proprietors. Bank failures of this sort were not uncommon in the 18th and 19th centuries until the emergence of the large joint-stock banks with many branches brought an element of stability into banking.

The failure of Messers Palmer & Greene was of quite a different sort, however. For nearly a century, under the name of the Lichfield Bank, the business which they owned had supplied the banking needs of Lichfield. Originally owned by the firm of Scott & Palmer, it had built up a reputation for reliability and integrity. They numbered among their customers the Corporation of Lichfield, the Conduit Lands Trust, the Dean and Chapter, the Staffordshire Yeomanry and Staffordshire Militia, the Union Work-house, the Lichfield Savings Bank and most of the gentry and tradesmen of the city.

Of the two partners, Richard Greene was the better-known in the Lichfield community. His grandfather, also named Richard Greene, had achieved fame in the days of Dr Johnson as the owner of the well-known "Museum of Curiosities". Coming to Lichfield in 1742 from Shrewsbury, where he had served his apprenticeship, he established himself as a surgeon-apothecary in premises in Market Street, where he displayed the traditional red and blue glass panes in his window. Here he had set up his museum which achieved national fame through the pages of the *Gentleman's Magazine*. In due course the collection passed to Greene's son-in-law, and on his death was broken up and sold, but two of the larger exhibits still remain today. One, " an organ, built originally by Father Smith, for the use of the Cathedral Church of Lichfield," after many vicissitudes arrived back at the Cathedral and in recent years was restored to be used as a chamber organ on suitable occasions. The other, a " curious clock " is now to be seen in Bath Museum, but unfortunately, unlike the organ, it no longer functions.

Richard Greene claimed relationship with Dr Johnson, but was never able to prove this connection.

His grandson will be already well-known to readers of this book. He was, it will be remembered, Chairman of the Railway Committee of 1836, a Director of the South Staffordshire Railway Company and originator of the heraldic designs on the railway bridge in St John Street. In later years he had become a Director of the South Staffordshire Waterworks Company and was closely associated with Chawner and McClean in their various projects. He was also the owner of collieries at Brownhills and Pelsall.

His home was at Stowe House, near St Chad's Church and overlooking Stowe Pool (ideally suited for following the progress of the waterworks!). Here he and his wife Mary lived in very comfortable circumstances with their five children and Richard Greene indulged in his interests of collecting rare books and breeding exotic fowl. In Lichfield he was connected with various voluntary organisations, being Chairman of the Lichfield Working Men's Association, Trustee of the Conduit Lands Trust, a member of the Board of Guardians and a Churchwarden of neighbouring St Chad's Church.

He had acquired his partnership in the bank through marriage, his wife having been formerly Mary Scott, daughter of one of the original partners. In this way the name of the firm changed from Scott & Palmer to Palmer & Greene.

It is evident that with all his other commitments Richard Greene had left the banking interest in the hands of James Palmer, who lived over the bank in Market Street and managed the day to day running of it. When Palmer died in 1850 it was found that he owed the bank £60,000 which his estate was quite unable to repay. It was a considerable sum for a small business in those days, and it must have been a great shock for Richard Greene. After taking legal advice, however, he found that as his total assests still exceeded the bank's liabilities he was able to carry on the banking business, and this he proceeded to do. But the business did not prosper as he hoped; perhaps the death of Palmer had caused a lack of confidence, or perhaps it was due to competition from the newly-opened branch of the National Provincial Bank of England at Number 1, Bird Street. The crisis came in December, 1855. The Lichfield Bank drew on Messers Smith, Payne & Smith of London, whose names appeared on their bank-notes as the persons who would exchange the notes for gold. Towards the end of the month, following the conveyance of a house, the large sum of £1,600 in Palmer & Greene's notes was paid into Messers Smith, Payne & Smith. The latter, fearing a run was about to start on the Lichfield Bank, sent for Richard Greene to give them a statement of his affairs. As a result they withdrew all their credit facilities without which he could not continue. From London he telegraphed to the bank, and at 3.0 p.m. on Monday, 31st December, the following notice appeared on the door of the premises in Market Street:

" LICHFIELD BANK

It is with deep concern that I find myself compelled to close the door of this establishment. The circumstances which occasion this necessity are remote, and will be fully explained without delay.

Richard Greene."

Lichfield soon learned that the circumstances were that Richard Greene had been compelled to file a petition in bankruptcy. Consequently the bank was closed and all the accounts frozen until the Bankruptcy Court had investigated the unfortunate Mr Greene's affairs. The consternation and distress in the city can be imagined. The Corporation were unable to draw on the product of their three-penny rate; half-pay officers of the Militia and Yeomanry were unable to draw their half-pay; hundreds of persons and businesses had to borrow to meet their immediate requirements and were left wondering how much of their deposits would be returned to them eventually. Even the Customs and Excise Office in Lichfield was unable to remit its collections to London, though it is doubtful if any tears were shed in Lichfield on that account. The one consolation was for depositors in the Lichfield Savings Bank, the Manager of which, Mr Allen, was able to assure them that as most of their savings were invested in Government Stock, the loss from Palmer & Greene's collapse would be minimal.

One can well imagine the gossip, rumours and speculation produced in the city by the failure of the bank, but much more was to follow. The story which unfolded would have been a worthy subject for the pen of Anthony Trollope.

On the 14th of January, 1856, Mr Bittleston, the Official Assignee appointed by the Birmingham Bankruptcy Court, came to Lichfield to examine the books of the Lichfield Bank. At lunchtime he and Mr Greene went to the George Hotel, together with Mr William Lawton, Mr Greene's Confidential Clerk. Lawton whom the *Staffordshire Advertiser* later described as " a venerable old man of 73 " had worked for the Bank for 35 years. A bachelor, he had a salary of £400 per annum (quite a substantial income in those days), lived comfortably in his Bird Street lodgings and was well-known and respected in the city.

In the course of the luncheon Mr Bittleston remarked that during the afternoon he would like to look at the records of the issue and withdrawal of the firm's bank-notes. It is not recorded at what point in the meal he made this announcement, but it is a fairly safe guess that from then on little interest was taken in what they were eating and drinking. For this was the cue for which

Mr Lawton had been waiting, and to a thunder-struck Mr Greene he announced that for the last six years he had been embezzling the bank's funds.

From the illustration of one of Palmer & Greene's bank-notes it will be seen that Lawton was responsible for issuing the notes. (His signature appears in the bottom left-hand corner). At the same time he entered on the note, in manuscript, the number and the date of issue and of course made an entry in the appropriate account book. Similarly, when notes became too worn or dirty for further use, he was responsible for withdrawing them, cancelling them by snipping off the top left-hand corner with the number on it, and making a contra entry in the account book. All he had done was to avoid cutting the numbers off the worn notes as they came to him and using them for his own purposes. It is an interesting comment on the state of affairs in Palmer & Greene's Bank that he had been able to do this for six years without it coming to light, when the simplest of checks would have shown it, and significant that he had started his embezzlement just before the death of Mr Palmer.

It is not difficult to imagine the feelings of Richard Greene when he realised that not only was he ruined financially, but that he had been betrayed by a trusted and long-serving employee. As for Mr Bittleston, he insisted on William Lawton accompanying him back to Birmingham the same day to make a statement to Mr Registrar Waterfield at the Bankruptcy Court. As Lawton left the court he was arrested by Inspector Glossop of the Birmingham Police and taken to the Police cells. From here he wrote to his former employer as follows:

" To R. Greene Esq.

Sir,

I have been given into custody for embezzlement, and having no desire to give the prosecution any trouble in the matter beg to declare that I have taken or abstracted from the cancelled notes of Messers Palmer & Greene, from time to time since 1849, the amount of £7,350 the bulk of which I have applied to assist a person in a lawsuit, which I fully expected to be settled long since and to be enabled to replace the money so abstracted, and never intended to defraud the Bank of one farthing.

Yours etc.

William Lawton."

The following day Mr Lawton was taken back to Lichfield where he appeared before Mr Thomas Adie, the Mayor, and Mr Hewitt J.P. He was remanded in custody until a further hearing on 26th January, at which he was committed to the next Lichfield Quarter Sessions.

While Mr Lawton was appearing for the second time before the Lichfield magistrates, the unfortunate Mr Greene was giving an account of his affairs in the Birmingham Bankruptcy Court. His liabilities, it seems, amounted to £180,000. All of this amount was connected with his banking activities—£74,500 deposited with him in current accounts, £91,500 in deposit accounts and a further estimated figure of £14,000 for bank-notes in circulation. The true figure for this last item would not, of course, be known till the full extent of Mr Lawton's activities was discovered.

Against these liabilities Mr Greene had but £121,000 worth of assets, even including his personal property such as Stowe House and the farm attached. One of the assets was £30,600 owed by sundry debtors on overdrawn accounts at the bank, which suggests that the citizens of Lichfield enjoyed very liberal credit facilities.

With such a state of affairs there was no hope of avoiding bankruptcy. One can imagine the feelings of Richard Greene and his family as they realised their situation. In 1856 to become bankrupt meant not only losing almost everything one posessed (the law allowed a bankrupt to keep for his own use the tools of his trade and the wearing apparel of himself, his wife and his children to an amount not exceeding in value the sum of £20), but it also carried a social stigma unknown today. One day Mr Greene and his wife Mary were respected members of Lichfield society, prosperous and comfortable in one of the most pleasantly situated houses in Lichfield. The next day they were little better off than the paupers in the Union Workhouse over which Mr Greene had presided as one of the Board of Guardians. The only hope for them was a complete break with Lichfield and an attempt to start a new life elsewhere at the age of 56.

For their son Richard, aged 28, life would not be too bad. After public school and three years at Oriel College Oxford he had returned to Lichfield with his B.A. to enter his father's bank with a view, no doubt, of taking it over in due course. Life would be a good deal harder, of course, but he was still young enough to make a new start in life. But for his sisters Caroline (23) and Georgina (19) their world had really been shattered. As daughters of a bankrupt their chances of making a " good " marriage were negligible, and for young ladies of their class opportunities for work just did not exist.

For all the family it meant that their comfortable existence at Stowe House with eight servants to look after their wants had come to an end. The last act in the tragedy was the selling up of the family home, that situation so dear to the hearts of Victorian novelists and genre painters. It came about towards the end of March, and the auctioneer's advertisements tell their own story. Stowe House was bought for £4,860 by a Dr Holland.

STOWE HOUSE, LICHFIELD

TO be SOLD by AUCTION by Mr. HARRIS, at the SWAN HOTEL, LICHFIELD, on Monday, the 31st day of March, 1856, at two o'clock in the afternoon, by order of the Assignees of Mr. Richard Greene, bankrupt, in one or more lots, as may be arranged at the time of sale, and subject to conditions of sale which will be then produced, all that MANSION HOUSE called " Stowe House," situated in the county of the city of Lichfield, comprising dining and drawing rooms, library, study, six good sized bedrooms and eight smaller rooms, two water closets, servant's hall, housekeeper's room, bakehouse, brewhouse, laundry, dairy, farm buildings and loose boxes five stalled stable, double and single coach-houses and other convenient offices conservatory, very complete fowl houses, with hot water apparatus. The premises are well supplied with excellent water.

This residence is most delightfully situated, nearly adjoining to Stowe Church, and commands views of the Cathedral Church and other objects of interest. The house is surrounded by a lawn well planted with shrubs flower and kitchen garden, with two forcing houses and bricked hot bed.

The Lichfield Station of the Trent Valley Railway is about one mile from Stowe, and that of the South Staffordshire Railway is about half-a-mile.

The House and 10A. 3R. 38P of Land near and adjoining to the house, are freehold, and the remaining lands also adjoining and near to the house, containing 13A. 1R. 27P., are held under the Sub-Chanter and Vicars Choral of the Cathedral Church of Lichfield on leases, usually renewed on reasonable terms.

Further particulars may be had, and a plan of the Estate may be seen, on application to Mr. THOMAS HODSON, Lichfield, and Messrs. MOTTERAM and KNIGHT, Birmingham, Solicitors to the Assignees; or to the AUCTIONEER, Lichfield, who will give tickets to view the premises.

STOWE HOUSE, LICHFIELD

Mr. HARRIS begs to announce that he has received instructions from the Assignees of the Estate of Mr. Richard Greene, banker to SUBMIT by AUCTION, on Tuesday, the 1st day of April next, and eleven following days (Sunday excepted), the whole of the rich and elegant FURNITURE, a beautiful carved Oak Chamber Suite, fine toned repetition GRAND PIANOFORTE, by Broadwoods; double-action HARP, by Erards; richly embossed and chased PLATE, PLATED GOODS, CUT GLASS, CHINA, LINEN; Cellar of OLD WINE, containing upwards of 350 dozen of the choicest vintages, including the most rare, curious, and expensive wines of the Continent. The Library consists of BOOKS of great interest, value, and rarity, among which are Musée Royal et Francais, six vols., a picked copy and splendidly bound; rare books of the period of Mary Queen of Scots, Old Poetry, Sicera Tracts, a large quantity of painter's etchings, prints, and books of prints; valuable PAINTINGS, by the first masters; handsome CARRIAGES; Cochin China, Dorking, Silver Hamburgh, and Silver-pencil FOWLS; and upwards of 600 GREENHOUSE PLANTS, upon the said premises.

ORDER OF SALE: —

First Day—Garden, conservatory, saddle-room, and stable.

Second Day—Kitchen, dining-room, chintz bedroom, and dressing-room.

Third Day—Housekeeper's-room, entrance-hall, staircase, drawing-room, best bedroom, and dressing-room.

Fourth Day—Rich cut glass, china and linen.

Fifth Day—Scullery, larder, dairy, study, library, oak bed chamber, and drab bedroom.

Sixth Day—Books.

Seventh Day—Books.

Eighth Day—Prints.

Ninth Day—Embossed plate, and paintings.

Tenth Day—Wine, and carriages.

Eleventh Day—Servants' hall, butler's pantry, back landing, green bed chamber, ladies' maid's bedroom, housemaid's bedroom, and upper landing.

Twelfth Day—Housemaid's closet, second chintz dressing-room, coachman's room, brewhouse, and workshop.

Particulars will be fully expressed in catalogue, which may be obtained of Mr. LOMAX, Bookseller, Bird-street; and of the AUCTIONEER, Market-place, Lichfield, fourteen days previous to the sale; price 1s. each, which will be returned to the purchasers.

The whole will be on view by cards only, which will be given by the AUCTIONEER, one week previous to the sale.

The Staffordshire Advertiser, Saturday, March 29, 1856.

And what of the wretched William Lawton? He appeared before the Recorder at Lichfield Quarter Sessions on 1st July. He pleaded " Not Guilty " and the case against him proceeded. Evidence was given by Richard Greene and his son, and by one of the other clerks, Cornelius Amsden. William Bodill, a messenger of the Bankruptcy Court testified that on searching Mr Lawton's lodgings he had found a number of bank-notes and a piece of paper, which was produced to the court, on which was written " Mrs B. £6,458; self £891.10s."

When Mr Lawton gave his evidence the whole sad story emerged. Mrs B. was the friend who had been carrying on a case in the Court of Chancery to lay claim to an alleged inheritance. As so often happened the case had dragged on for years, and to finance the litigation William Lawton had embezzled his employer's funds, hoping all the time for the successful conclusion which never came—the case of " Jarndyce v Jarndyce " over again. Not only Trollope, but also Charles Dickens would have appreciated the story of the Lichfield Bank.

At the end of the report of the trial, in the Calendar of the Lichfield Quarter Sessions, the Clerk to the Court has pencilled in, after the names of the witnesses, " Josiah Bartlett and Elizabeth his wife were also called, but did not answer."

Was Elizabeth Bartlett the mysterious " Mrs B. " of the note? If so she proved a very false friend, deserting William Lawton in his hour of trial. Both Trollope and Dickens would have drawn a very suitable moral from the story.

The old man was found guilty and sentenced to four years penal servitude. He was taken down stairs from the courtroom in Lichfield Guildhall to the Gaol and House of Correction below. The cells which he and the other inmates inhabited are still there, used today as storerooms by the Lichfield District Council. In the yard outside, where William Lawton and countless other prisoners over the years took their exercise, councillors now park their cars.

Another court case which excited tremendous interest in Lichfield in the year 1856 was the case of Swinfen versus Swinfen. Because it involved a widowed woman and her fight for justice, almost on her own, against the full might of the English legal system, it attracted national interest. The story of Patience Swinfen, the Lichfield widow, is told in a succeeding chapter.

May, 1856 saw the ending the campaign in the Crimea, and in common with other towns throughout the kingdom Lichfield celebrated peace with great rejoicings.

In 1854 twenty-seven men from Lichfield had gone to the war with the 13th Light Dragoons. They had taken part in the never-to-be-forgotten charge of the Light Brigade at Balaclava. Now only four of them were returning. One of these was Trumpeter Browne who had sounded the " Charge " on that memorable occasion. He lived to a peaceful old age and now lies buried in St Michael's churchyard, with his trumpet beside him.

The Town Council had decided to leave the consideration of the Peace Celebrations to a public meeting, and this was held on 21st May with the Mayor, Mr Adie, in the chair. It was resolved that there should be a procession, a dinner, tea meetings in various parts of the town and a ball at the Guildhall. A committee was set up, subscriptions invited, and the Mayor headed the list with £5. In a very short time £155 had been raised.

It was generally agreed that the resulting celebrations " surpassed anything of the kind for the last forty years,"* which took one back to the Battle of Waterloo. The procession started in Bore Street and moved along the route of St John Street, Bird Street, Beacon Street, The Close, Dam Street, Tamworth Street, George Lane, Lombard Street finishing in the Market Place. It consisted of : —

Citizen on Horseback

Children of Lichfield Union (the Workhouse)

Children of the National Schools

Christ Church School

St Mary's School

---

* *Staffordshire Advertiser.*

St Chad's School (Stowe)

Minor's Grammar School

Private Schools

King Edward VI Grammar School

Lichfield Licensed Victuallers Association

Militia Band

Companies of Militia

Crimean Ambulance, drawn by two horses, with heroes inside

The Friendly Institution

Loyal Brunswick Lodge (Oddfellows)

Lodge of the Wolverhampton Unity

Lodge of the Manchester Unity

Band of Music

City Dozeners (with Flags)

Police

Gaoler and Sheriff's Officer

Town Crier

Sergeants at Mace

Mayor

High Sheriff

Aldermen

Citizens

Harmonic Band

Companies of Militia

Altogether 1,400 schoolchildren took part and there would probably be a similar number of adults. It will be noted that the procession must have passed itself on two occasions, so the whole event would have been quite a feat of organisation. The ambulance was supplied by Messers Holmes, Coachmakers, who had a manufactury in Bore Street where presumably they had been making these useful vehicles.

On arrival at the Market Square the Militia were drawn up in line and the others assembled. The Mayor then read the Queen's proclamation, " God Save the Queen " was played by the Harmonic Band and three volleys were fired by the Militia. Then the National Anthem was repeated by the Militia Band, three cheers were given for the Queen, and the company departed.

The children went to their respective schools to be entertained with tea parties, while the men received their refreshment in the Corn Exchange and Market Hall and the " fair sex " held tea drinkings in the various wards. The inmates of the workhouse were regaled with " an ample supply of provisions," whatever that might mean.

Flags and banners and evergreens decorated most of the houses in the town, and Mr Alsop in Tamworth Street flew a flag made from the jackets of some of those who had fallen in battle during the campaign. (One cannot help wondering where he got these from). As darkness fell the city was illuminated with special displays lit by gas. Messers Garratt & Chambers had a Brunswick Star composed of 360 lights, there was another star over the premises of Mr Perks, a huge V.R. in lights over the coach manufactury of Mr Holmes in Bore Street and another V.R. over Mr Gilliard's in the Market Place. At the Swan sixty gentlemen sat down to dinner and at the Guildhall a grand ball went on into the early hours of the morning, while the public houses were thronged with citizens and country folk who had come in to see the lights.

It was fortunate that the celebrations took place when they did and not a few weeks later, for on 29th July the city was rocked by a violent explosion in the Gas Works at Sandford Street. It took place late in the evening, and the lights went out all over Lichfield. The Conduit Lands Trust manual fire engine was despatched from its house below the Guildhall, but fortunately was not required, for although there was a very great escape of gas there was no fire. The explosion had taken place in the refining house, the roof of which had been blown off.

Before leaving the subject of the law, mention must be made of one more case—a relatively insignificant one compared with those already mentioned. It attracted little attention and rated only a single paragraph in the press, yet its social significance was considerable. In the same paper that reported the Swinfen case it was also mentioned that at Lichfield Petty Sessions Francis Sharratt Burnett, chimney sweep, had been summonsed by Mr Peter Hall for employing a boy to sweep a chimney. It was a reminder of the times, not long past, when " climbing boys " were sent up chimneys to sweep them; the days of Charles Kingsley's " Water Babies " and a practice now banned by law.

In this case it transpired that the boy had been placed in the sweep's care by his mother, a strolling player, when he was four years old—a not-uncommon situation. The magistrates dismissed the case on the grounds that the boy had not been ill-treated, but Mr Francis Eggington Jnr, the owner of the house, was fined five shillings for allowing the boy to climb the chimney.

Another, but very different, sign of the growing enlightment of the age that took place in that year was the decision by the Corporation to build a public library. At first sight this may not appear a very momentous decision, but in fact it was. The year before, Mr Ewart had piloted through Parliament his Public Libraries Act which made available to municipal corporations money with which to build public libraries. The first authority to use this power was Manchester—they put up a small building in the classical style, a model of which can be seen today in Manchester Central Library.

The second city to avail itself of this right was Lichfield, and the resulting building was the one which, unlike Manchester, we still use today. Its provision is often attributed to the Lichfield Conduit Lands Trust, but for once that admirable body were not involved. Credit must go to the Corporation, urged on by that benefactor of the city, Chancellor James Thomas Law. During the summer of 1856 entries were invited from achitects in competition, and by December the press reported that " entries had been received from all over the country." The design eventually chosen was that of Messers Bidlake & Lovatt of Wolverhampton, and the building contract went to Messers Lilley of the same town.

The laying of the foundation stone took place on 3rd October, 1857, and was considered important enough for an article in the *Illustrated London News.* " A very large procession was formed at the Guildhall at noon," it was reported, " headed by the Mayor and Corporation, magistrates, dignitaries of the Cathedral and a large number of citizens. The magnificent band of the King's Own Staffordshire Militia was in attendance. On arrival at the site the Chairman of the Library Committee (John P. Dyott Esq) presented the Rev Thomas Law, Chancellor of the Diocese, with a beautiful silver trowel, requesting him, in the name of the citizens, to lay the foundation stone. The Chancellor, having performed the ceremony, made an admirable address after which an eloquent speech and prayers were delivered by the Venerable Archdeacon Moore. Then Lord Alfred Paget, M.P., addressed the assemblage; the inauguration being closed by the performance of the Grand Chorus from ' The Creation ' by the band and the cheers of the vast multitude. The whole of those present then attended a sumptuous luncheon in the Guildhall."

The article was illustrated with the architect's drawing of the proposed building, showing it very much as we know it today, except for the heavy buttresses which now disfigure it. These were added in the present century to correct the effects of subsidence caused by the soft nature of the soil at this point. Describing it the writer went on to add, " The building is beautifully situated at the end of the bridge in Bird Street, near to the west gate of the cathedral and close to the foundations of an ancient tower which some centuries ago stood on the margin of the great pool. The library and reading room will be on the ground floor and the whole of the first floor will be the museum. In the basement will be exhibition rooms for the sculpture etc. and the hall keeper's residence.

The entrance is by a high and handsome tower, looking over the monster* pool and up Bird Street, having ornamental grounds in front of upwards of two acres. The material used in the construction are tinted white bricks with dressings of Bath stone."

Lichfield's Library and Museum can truthfully be described as an exciting building—in its time it has excited admiration, alarm (when it was discovered to be sinking), horror and even mirth (in his book on Staffordshire in the Buildings of England series, Nikolaus Pevsner describes it as " funny "). In its original form, without the buttresses, it is a straightforward example of the Italianiate style that was so popular in England in the 1860's following its introduction into this country by Prince Albert when he himself used it for the design of Osborne House, on the Isle of Wight, for Queen Victoria and their family. The popularity of the style was confined largely to the south of England and especially to seaside resorts such as Torquay and was unusual as far north as Lichfield; hence the reason why it looks out of place. There is no other building of this style in Lichfield. Probably we owe it to the taste of Chancellor Law.

Today the first floor acts as an art gallery, for in spite of its historic past Lichfield seems to be incapable of sustaining a museum. Whether the basement ever housed any exhibitions of sculpture as proposed is doubtful, but at least the city has two very pleasant pieces of 18th century Italian work today. These came from Swinfen Hall and were an example of the generosity of Colonel Swinfen-Broun towards the people of Lichfield. One of them will be familiar to all those who use the library; the charming figure of the young girl who sits in the foyer for ever braiding her hair and looking at the book on her lap—a very appropriate subject for a library, though to be sure the young lady wears less clothes than are usual for either readers or librarians. The other statue, of another young girl holding back as Father Time tries to drag her forward, is unfortunately no longer on view.

Less attractive, but more mysterious, is the figure of the sailor who mounts guard to the left of the main entrance. He would appear to date from the Boer War period; his cap-ribbon is

---

* A printers error, we imagine. No prizes are given for the correct answer!

inscribed " H.M.S. Powerful," he is dressed in field-service order and at one time he carried a Lee-Enfield rifle, Mark I (now reduced by vandals to the semblance of a sawn-off shotgun). Who is he? Who put him there? Alas, there is no inscription, no identification whatever. We are left wondering at the story behind it.

1856 was also the Year of The Clock. The demolition of the tower of St Mary's Church had left the city without any public clock near its centre. St Michael's had one, but that was some way out of town; the Cathedral had a striking clock, but this had no exterior dials. Moreover, this lack of public timepiece coincided with a general passion throughout the country for horological exactitude. Up to the middle of the 19th Century towns and cities all over the land had kept their own time, which was sometimes as much as ten minutes either side of London time. The invention of the electric telegraph by Cooke and Wheatstone in 1837, and its rapid spread throughout the kingdom had made exact Greenwich time available in every town. The Victorian zest for scientific advance seized upon this possibility, and the result was the rash of Victorian Gothic clock towers which appeared at this time.

The possession of such a clock tower was a matter of civic pride, and there was no lack of that in Lichfield. The Corporation were urged to do something about it, and as usual there were plenty of people who knew exactly what should be done. One correspondent in the "Staffordshire Advertiser" (5th May) even suggested that the proposed clock should be illuminated by electric light. And this in 1856!

As to who should meet the cost, it was unanimously agreed that those Universal Aunts, the Conduit Lands Trustees, should have that privilege. The Trustees accordingly deliberated and came up with the idea for a clock-tower in the Market Place. The proposed erection was to consist of a Neo-Gothic canopy over the statue of Samuel Johnson, buttressed, pinnacled and crocketed in approved style and obviously inspired by the memorial to Sir

Walter Scott in Prince's Street, Edinburgh, erected some twelve
years earlier. Beneath this stately pile Sam Johnson would sit and
brood, while time passed by over his head on four small dials.*

The proposal was received favourably and almost put into
effect. Mercifully, however, it was dropped, but it is interesting to
note that some years later a similar design (but without the clocks)
was adopted for the memorial to Prince Albert in Kensington
Gardens—now one of London's best-known landmarks!

Instead of the Johnson Memorial Clock an entirely different
plan was followed. At the junction of St John Street and Bore
Street stood the Crucifix Conduit, the original mediaeval water
supply of the city. Now that water was piped throughout the city,
the original conduits were no longer required. The Market Cross
Conduit, was accordingly demolished; so too was the Butcher Row
Conduit, though the site of the latter was commemorated by
changing the name of Butcher Row into " Conduit Street." The
third conduit, the Stone Cross Conduit, at the Junction of
Tamworth and Lombard Streets, was also removed and the same
fate would have befallen the Crucifix Conduit if the Trustees had
not hit on the happy idea of using it for the base of the clock tower.
Joseph Potter, Junior, was the architect selected, and he produced
a Norman design for the tower (a reference, perhaps, to the ancient
origins of the conduit). No time was lost in getting on with the
building, and it was completed within twelve months at a cost of
£1,200.

The fitting up of the timepiece took much longer however. In
his " History of the Conduit Lands Trust," Percy Laithwaite
describes the difficulties and delays as follows:

" In February, 1864 the Clock Committee passed a resolution
that the clock should strike the quarters on two bells; in March that
it should strike the Cambridge chimes and have three dials, the one

---

* This was probably the idea of Chancellor Law, the donor of the statue.
His ambition to present a public clock was realised, however in 1864
when he designed a mausoleum in St. Michael's Churchyard, for his wife
and himself. This had a clock on top of it, illuminated by gas. The
mausoleum can still be seen, opposite St Michael's Rectory, with the gas
pipe still running into it, but the clock has long-since been removed.

facing west being deemed unnecessary; in April, following a protest from the tenant of the Friary, that there should be four dials. In September they engaged John Gilbert, Junior, to attend to the winding of the long-awaited timepiece, but alas, in October they refused to accept the clock when delivered on the grounds that although they paid £300 for it, it was a five-day instead of an eight-day clock, its chimes were defective and no guarantee was forthcoming as to its accuracy.

" A succession of operators having all failed to cope with the wayward timepiece, it was eventually entrusted to that renowned Lichfield clockmaker, Thornelow, who put it to right for £7 10s. 0d. and kept it in good going order for many years."

To illuminate it at night the Trustees first placed a reflecting oil lamp on the building on the opposite side of the road (the Talbot Inn, which stood at the corner of Bore Street and Bird Street), but this only illuminated one dial. In 1882 the experiment was tried of painting the dials black and the hands and figures with luminous paint. This does not seem to have been very successful, however, for a few years later the present glass dials were fitted, illuminated from inside by gas burners. This must have proved too expensive, for after a short time smaller burners were fitted and the one on the west side removed altogether—no doubt once again to the complaint of the one household in the Friary!

In 1926, when the present road through the Friary was made, the clocktower stood right in the way. Lichfield Corporation bought it from the Conduit Lands for £50 and demolished it, and that might have been the end of one of Lichfield's best-known landmarks. But a rescuer appeared in the person of Sir Richard Cooper of Shenstone who paid the cost of moving the tower and rebuilding it in its present position by the Bowling Green Inn. And there it stands today after many vicissitudes, a monument to the endeavours of those who over many centuries worked " for the commonweal of the city," and a useful time-check for the motorists speeding past on their way to Birmingham, Walsall or Stafford.

CHAPTER VIII

A Lady and the Law
The Case of
Swinfen v. Swinfen

In the last chapter mention was made of the Swinfen lawsuit, or to be more exact, lawsuits, for this case which attracted nation-wide attention took place, in all its ramifications, over a period of eight years during which there were hearings in the Archbishop of Canterbury's Prerogative Court, The Court of Common Pleas (twice), Stafford Assizes, Warwick Assizes, the Court of the Exchequer and the Court of Chancery. Reading the accounts of it is almost a guide to the judicial system of England in the 19th century.

The litigation centred around the estate of Swinfen, in the parish of Weeford, about two and a half miles south of Lichfield on the London Road. In 1856 it consisted of 1,243 acres and included four farms; Whitehouse Farm, Horseley Brook Farm, Ingley Hill Farm, and The Home Farm which stood just by the the main entrance to Swinfen Hall. The Hall itself was a fine country mansion built for the Swinfen family in 1755 by the architect Benjamin Wyatt, father of James Wyatt.* In its original state it was a symmetrical building of red brick with much stone dressing, of seven bays and two and a half storeys, surmounted all the way round by a stone balustrade.

---

* See Chapter I.

It was a typical country gentleman's seat of the time, set in a pleasant landscape of rolling countryside alongside a lake and surrounded by fine timber.

The Swinfen family had held the estate for several centuries; in the seventeenth century a John Swinfen, a Parliamentary supporter, had sat in the Long Parliament. Then, in 1767, the estate came into the possesion of one John Grundy by way of a marriage settlement. He changed his name to Swinfen and came to live at Swinfen Hall, where he continued his main interests of horse racing and betting. A reminder of this is a handsome silver trophy which today forms part of Lichfield's civic plate. It takes the form of a large silver-gilt cup and cover in the Adam style embossed with the figure of a racehorse and dated 1780. With it is a letter from John Swinfen to Lord de Ferrers of Chartley, challenging him to a race on Whittington Heath. Presumably John Swinfen's horse won on that occasion, for the cup was later presented to the Mayor and Corporation of Lichfield by a member of the Swinfen family.

Not all his sporting activities were as successful, however, and when his son Samuel succeeded to the estate in 1828 he found it to be heavily mortgaged. Most of the furniture in the Hall had been sold, and the wine cellar, in his own words, contained " only half a gallon of sour beer and a bottle of soda water."

Samuel himself had been no sluggard when it came to getting rid of money; in 1795 he had married Susannah, daughter of Sir Thomas Durrant of Norwich, who brought with her a fortune of £20,000. By the time he inherited the Swinfen estate he had managed to dispose of all this by gambling and reckless speculation. Fortunately his wife had more backbone; although the daughter of a baronet she set to and did all the housework of the Hall while they lived in one room.* She also took over the management of the Home Farm and grew to like farming so much that in the latter part of her life she was interested in little else. She and her husband led a frugal life; they wore the clothes of people engaged

---

* The one on the right as one enters the Hall.

in agriculture and every Friday Samuel Swinfen, in his working clothes, walked the two-and-a-half miles to Lichfield Market and back and ate his dinner at the Market Table.

They had little or no social life and few amusements, but by the time Susannah died in 1848 they had, largely through her efforts, put the estate back on something like a sound footing and paid off the mortgages.

Of their two children one, a daughter, died in infancy. Their only son, Henry John, was a rather colourless character who did little in his lifetime except contract a marriage which upset his family.

In 1831 Samuel Swinfen and Henry were in London, engaged in proceedings in the Court of Chancery connected with the mortgages. They lodged at the boarding house of a Miss Ayres at 63 Russell Square, and here Henry took a fancy to one of Miss Ayres parlour-maids, Patience Williams.

As Patience is to become the heroine of this story, some mention of her should be made here. She was born in the little town of Llanfair Caerinion, Montgomeryshire,* the daughter of a yeoman. Her portrait, painted in her middle age by Samuel West, shows her as a very handsome woman, dark-haired and with typical Welsh features. One can easily imagine how attractive she must have been at the age of eighteen when she stole the heart of Henry Swinfen. He was twenty-nine at the time.

But Patience had many more qualities than just a pretty face. She was intelligent, generous and kind to her friends (but implacable to her enemies), but above all full of a determination to succeed that was quite lacking in the men of the Swinfen family. It was this determination to get on in the world that took Patience and her sister Margaret from the backwoods of Montgomeryshire to the great metropolis while both were still in their teens. It was no doubt this determination to succeed that impelled Patience to respond to Henry's advances. What happened then was described by Miss Ayres' niece many years later in the following words.

---

* Well-known today to railway enthusiasts as the home of a light railway.

Recalling Patience, she said, " she came to us with a very good reference. Miss Ayres was much distressed by Mr Henry Swinfen's attentions to Patience, and spoke to his father about it, who said that she was a very fine girl, that his son was quite right to look after her, and he would not mind having her himself. To this Miss Ayres replied she was sure that something disagreeable would happen."

What did happen was that one Sunday Patience and Henry John slipped away to St Paul's Church, Bloomsbury, and were united in Holy Matrimony. They did not return to Russell Square and the news of the wedding was brought back by one of Henry's friends.

Whatever Samuel Swinfen may have felt about his son's wife (and he always had an eye for a good-looking female, right to the end of his days), his feelings were not shared by Henry's mother. Whatever the station in life that she had been forced to adopt, she could not forget that she was a baronet's daughter. She was not pleased with Henry's behaviour and would not receive the couple at Swinfen. But Henry could afford to be independent; at the age of twenty-one his father had settled on him £360 a year from the estate with a further £300 when he married. This Henry now claimed and with quite a comfortable income for those days they spent the next eight years living in France and Italy where Patience's horizons were duly enlarged. Wherever they went she attracted the attention of men friends; she was one of those women who make friends easily with men of all ages. But she remained faithful to her Henry and was a dutiful wife. They never had any children.

In 1848 Susannah Swinfen died after a short illness, and from then on Samuel took little interest in the estate or in affairs outside. His only relatives were his half-brothers (old John Swinfen had married a second time),, and with these he had no contact. His only visitors were his physician, Dr Rowley of Lichfield, his attorney Charles Simpson,* his vicar the Rev. Robert Cowpland, and our old friend Richard Chawner of Wall who sometimes

---

* See Chapter III.

called on him. The old man was looked after by Mrs Elizabeth Martin, the wife of one of the gardeners, and she made the most of the opportunity to feather her own nest. So too did the many poachers who came on to the land with impunity. Once again the estate went to rack and ruin. Meanwhile Samuel Swinfen's health deteriorated until at last Dr Rowley felt it necessary to write to his son and advise him to come back to Swinfen.

When Henry and Patience arrived they found that as a result of a fall the old man was confined to his bedroom. It was the only one in the house that was furnished, and for some time they had to put up at the George Hotel in Lichfield and go out to Swinfen each day. But Patience soon took charge of the situation. She dismissed Mrs Martin, the dishonest servant, and engaged a reliable woman as nurse to her father-in-law and also a cook and a housemaid. She sent for a tailor from Lichfield to measure up Samuel for some new clothes and for an upholsterer to furnish a couple of rooms for herself and Henry. The latter purchased a phaeton and horse in which he used to drive his father into Lichfield and around the district on outings. There is no doubt that between them they rescued the old man from a stage of wretchedness, and equally there is little doubt that most of the credit for this was due to Patience. She gave him all the attention that could be expected from a dutiful daughter-in-law, visiting him daily and sitting with him and reading to him. Chaos gave way to order, and squalor to comfort. Before long Samuel Swinfen was not only reconciled to his son and daughter-in-law, but was imploring Patience not to leave him. So she and her husband stayed on, and all might have been well, for as the heir-in-law Henry Swinfen would automatically have inherited the estate on his father's death. But three years after their return to Swinfen, in June 1854, Henry once again caused a crisis in the affairs of the Swinfen family by inconsiderately dying while his father was still alive. It happened suddenly, after a short illness, and it was perhaps typical of Henry that his departure from this life caused much more stir than anything he had done while he was alive.

For the situation now arose that the new heir-in-law was one Captain Frederick Hay Swinfen, 5th Dragoon Guards, the son of the eldest of Samuel Swinfen's half-brothers and one of the relatives with whom the old man had had no contact for years. He had been very embittered towards his half-brothers, maintaining that they had in some way impoverished the Swinfen estate during his father's lifetime. Now one of their descendants would inherit Swinfen unless some action were taken, and there would be nothing for Patience.

To what extent Samuel appreciated the situation can only be guessed at, for he was now very feeble and near to his end. He had, however, on several occasions expressed his wish that the Swinfen estate should go to Patience on his death.

Staying at Swinfen Hall at this time were Charles Swinfen and his wife from Leamington. He was the only one of the half-brothers who had shown any interest in the relations at Swinfen, and he and his wife had come over for Henry's funeral and had stayed on to keep Patience company. They obviously grew to like her and sympathised with her position. So too did Dr and Mrs Rowley, and between them it was decided that Samuel Swinfen's wishes should be put into legal form. So Mr Charles Simpson was summoned from his office in Lichfield and the situation explained to him. He had not seen Samuel Swinfen for two years, and from accounts he had heard about his health doubted his ability to make a will. However, after a short talk with the old man his doubts were resolved and he retired to another room and drew up the following will:

" I, Samuel Swinfen of Swinfen Hall in the County of Stafford make this my last will and testament. I give to Mrs Taylor* who lives with me £20 a year for life. I give to Mrs Swinfen, my son's widow, all my estate at Swinfen or thereto adjoining also all furniture and other moveable goods here, to her, her heirs, executors, administrators and assigns, and I appoint her executrix.

Witness my hand this seventh day of July, 1854.

Signed . . ."

---

* Mr Swinfen's nurse.

Mr Swinfen signed the will with great difficulty; he could not hold the old-fashioned quill pen that was brought him, and even with Mr Simpson's modern steel-nibbed pen the best he could produce was something of a scrawl.   It was witnessed by Dr Rowley, by Charles Swinfen, and by Mr Simpson.

Nineteen days later, on 26th July, Samuel Swinfen died and Mrs Henry Swinfen became the châtelaine of Swinfen Hall.

She entered into her new role with zest.   She prosecuted the poachers, dismissed the idlers, chased up the debtors and began putting the estate on a sound footing.   Once again Swinfen had a hand at the helm and a female one at that, and for a time matters ran smoothly.

But not for long.   Captain Frederick Swinfen, the heir-at-law, had been consulting his legal advisers and during the course of the year 1855 Mrs Henry Swinfen received notification that the following cause had been entered for hearing at the Court of Chancery in London.

" Whereas Samuel Swinfen, late of Swinfen Hall in the County of Stafford, Esquire, was on the seventh of July, 1854, and from thence to the time of his death, seised in fee simple of a certain estate at Swinfen, and the said Samuel Swinfen died on the twenty-sixth of July, in the year 1854; whereupon Frederick Hay Swinfen the eldest son of Francis Swinfen, who was the eldest brother of the half-blood of the said Samuel Swinfen is the heir-at-law of the said Samuel Swinfen; and Patience Swinfen affirms and the said Frederick Hay Swinfen denies that the same Samuel Swinfen did by a certain writing bearing date the seventh day of July, 1854, purporting to be the last will and testament of the said Samuel Swinfen, devise the said estate at Swinfen, etc."

In the Court of Chancery the Master of the Rolls," desirous of ascertaining the truth by the verdict of a jury," referred the case to the Staffordshire Lent Assizes, where it opened before Mr Justice Cresswell on the 15th March, 1856.   Not surprisingly it created great interest locally and was widely covered in the press.

On the instructions of the Court of Chancery, Patience Swinfen appeared as Plaintiff and Captain Swinfen as Defendant. To put his case the Captain had retained the services of the Attorney General, Sir Alexander Cockburn Q.C., assisted by Mr Whateley Q.C., Mr Keating Q.C. and Mr Vaughan Richards. To put the case of Patience Swinfen, Charles Simpson, her attorney, had briefed Sir Frederick Thesiger Q.C., assisted by Mr Alexander Q.C. and Mr Whitmore Q.C.

At that time Sir Frederick Thesiger (later Lord Chelmsford) was at the height of a very successful career at the Bar. He was born in 1794, the son of a sugar planter who owned estates in St Vincent, West Indies, and grandson of a native of Saxony. Educated in England, he left school at the age of 13 to enter the Royal Navy as a midshipman, serving under Nelson at the Battle of Copenhagen. But after a short time, owing to the death of his elder brother, he became heir to the St Vincent estates and was accordingly withdrawn from the Navy and sent back to school. In 1812 he went out to St Vincent to learn the family business, but shortly after his arrival the eruption of a volcano obliterated the Thesiger estates. So back to England came Frederick to read law, being entered at Gray's Inn. He was called to the Bar in 1818 and practised in London. He became a K.C. in 1834 and shortly afterwards was elected a member of Parliament for the Woodstock Division, in the Conservative cause. In 1842 he was awarded the degree of Doctor of Common Law by the University of Oxford. He was described as " having a fine presence and handsome features, a pleasant if too frequent wit and the gift of natural eloquence." No doubt Charles Simpson felt that in securing the services of Sir Frederick he had done well by his client.

There is no doubt, however, that Sir Frederick suffered from two disadvantages common to successful barristers at that time. In the first place he tended to take on more work than he could reasonably attempt, and on this occasion, although the Swinfen case was due to open on a Saturday, he had another important case starting at Swansea on the following Tuesday. And secondly, he was too prone to regard his clients as mere ciphers who would accept whatever course of action he might suggest to them. In the case of Patience Swinfen this was a dangerous assumption.

The case opened at Stafford on Saturday, 13th March, 1856, at 10 o'clock before Mr Justice Cresswell and revolved around the argument as to whether the testator, Samuel Swinfen, had been of sound mind when he signed his last will and testament. The witnesses were those who had seen him in his last days; Mrs Taylor the nurse, Dr and Mrs Rowley, the Reverend Robert Cowpland and Mrs Swinfen herself. In the witness box, under cross-examination, they were no match for opposing counsel who made the most of every opportunity to question Samuel Swinfen's state of mind, a subject lending itself easily to ridicule. Only Patience Swinfen stood up well to questioning, although she was examined and cross-examined for three and a half hours. Poor Mr Cowpland came out of it worst. Describing one of his visits he explained that he had read the prayers for the visitation of the sick. The following ensued :

Learned Counsel.   " And what was Mr Swinfen's response to that?"

Mr Cowpland.   " He said ' Amen '."

Learned Counsel.   " Really!" (laughter in court).

Perhaps because of such exchanges an air of levity seems to have pervaded the court and led, late on Saturday afternoon, to the following rather extraordinary conversation :

Mr Justice Cresswell.   " How long is this case likely to last?"

Sir F. Thesiger.   " A long time."

Mr Justice Cresswell.   " In that case I will be obliged to do as was formerly done with refractory jury-men, viz., take them in a cart to the border of the county and shoot them out." (laughter).

During the day's proceedings Mr Justice Cresswell had several times shown signs of impatience and was obviously anxious to get the case over as soon a possible. When the court adjourned at six o'clock he was seen to beckon to Sir Frederick Thesiger who stood on a bench and carried on a short conversation with the judge. What passed between them is not known, but Sir Frederick then went and spoke to the Attorney General. Not long afterwards Mr Charles Simpson was called to Sir Frederick Thesiger's lodgings and it was put to him that the case was likely to go against them, that the other side had expressed a willingness to come to an arrangement and that it would be as well to do so. To this Mr Simpson replied, very properly, that he could say nothing until he had spoken to his client.

A messenger was then sent to Patience Swinfen who was dining at the Swan Inn, in the High Street, with Sir Henry Durrant, a relative of her mother-in-law. He had come over from Norwich for the case and had escorted Patience to Stafford. The message was a summons for Mrs Swinfen kindly to come to the lodgings of Sir Frederick.

On arrival there she found herself in the presence of the three counsel, Sir Frederick, Mr Whitmore and Mr Alexander. She was urged by Sir Frederick to agree to a settlement; he had been told he said " by the highest authority " that the case was going against them, but he believed that he could rescue £1,000 a year for Patience from the wreck. It was a tempting proposition for her; anyone of less resolution might have given way. But she replied that she wanted the case to go to a verdict; she would not compromise.

Sir Frederick repeated his proposals, " kicking his legs impatiently," and they urged her to accept. It was a daunting situation with three clever and experienced men of the law confronting the former parlour maid. Patience felt she needed some support and asked for Sir Henry Durrant to be sent for. This was agreed to, and when he came she said, " Now will you please repeat to this gentleman what you have said to me."

Nonplussed at first, Sir Henry turned to Patience and said, " I think we had better talk this over." So it was arranged that they should do so, and as they were returning to Swinfen that evening they would send the reply " by electric telegraph " the following day which was a Sunday.

On Sunday morning Mr Simpson came over to Swinfen and there was a long discussion. As a result a telegram was sent to Sir Frederick at Stafford with the message " Offer refused."

On Monday morning Patience and Sir Henry proceeded to Stafford by the first train from Lichfield, which arrived at ten o'clock. At nine o'clock the court had assembled and Sir Frederick got up to announce that the parties had agreed to a compromise, the details of which would be available in a very short time. While these were being put to paper, Mr Simpson begged Mr Justice Cresswell to hold up the proceedings until his client had arrived, which would be shortly after ten o'clock. But the judge refused, and at ten minutes to ten it was announced that an arrangement had been made whereby the estate was to be conveyed to Captain Frederick Swinfen and Mrs Henry Swinfen was to receive an annuity of £1,000 per annum charged upon the estate. The case was closed and the jury dismissed.

Minutes later Patience arrived at the courtroom, to find that the trial was over. She expressed herself astonished that a proposal which had been made to her counsel on Saturday and refused by her should be agreed to on Monday morning. Well might she be.

By the terms of the written agreement (which Patience refused to sign) she was to be allowed to stay at Swinfen Hall rent-free until Michaelmas. Promptly on 29th September Captain Frederick Swinfen, his mamma Mrs Francis Swinfen (who lost no opportunity of advancing her son's case) and their solicitor Mr Frere, arrived at Swinfen Hall. What happened was described thus in the *Staffordshire Advertiser*.

" The 29th ult, being the day fixed by the Court of Common Pleas on which Swinfen Hall and grounds were to be handed over to Captain Swinfen, the heir at law, the Captain proceeded in person to demand possession. He was not admitted, and after walking round the grounds retired, when Mrs Henry Swinfen, who had been watching the Captain's movements from the different windows of the house, opened one of them and discharged a pistol in the rear of the retreating captain, happily without effect. (Communicated)."

This brought the following rejoinder from Mrs. Swinfen, the next week:

THE SWINFEN ESTATE

To the EDITOR of the STAFFORDSHIRE ADVERTISER.

SIR—My attention has been called to a statement in your paper relating to me.

I was not aware that business of a private nature is within the scope of your vocation as a journalist.

It is a rare thing for a British officer to be scared by the blaze of gunpowder, much less by the innocent explosion of a *feu de joie*. It would appear from your report, which you state to have been *communicated* to you, though not by whom, that Captain Swinfen, a claimant of the Swinfen estate, came in person to demand possession, and was refused admittance to the mansion, and that a pistol was fired by me in his rear as he retreated, but *happily without effect*. Allow me through the medium of your columns to assure your readers that it would have been strange indeed if the discharge of the pistol could have been attended with any such effect as your correspondent insinuates; for it could hardly have had the effect of even shaking the nerves of the gallant captain, who had proceeded a considerable distance on his way out of the park, in company with his mother, his solicitor, and a stranger—not to mention that the little pistol was charged only with my thimbleful of powder and pointed in an opposite direction.

I remain, sir, your obedient servant,

PATIENCE SWINFEN.

Swinfen Hall, October 9th, 1856.

The battle was now on, and for the next two years Patience was to need all her determination and courage. She based her case on the simple fact that she had never agreed to the settlement, which had been entered into without her consent, and she therefore considered herself legally entitled to Swinfen Hall under the terms of Samuel Swinfen's will. In this she was fortunate in having the support of her attorney, Charles Simpson. Throughout his life he was always a champion of the underdog, and his sense of integrity and justice, for which he was renowned, was roused by the way in which his client had been treated by the legal profession.

Following the trial in March, an order of Nisi Prius had been served on Patience Swinfen by the Court of Common Pleas, which required her to carry out the terms of the agreement. This, as we have seen, she refused to do, and in June 1857 a Rule was obtained from the Court to show cause why she should not be attached for disobedience of the order. If she continued to disobey she could be imprisoned for contempt of court.

It was at this time that her affairs reached their lowest ebb. Not only was she harassed by the law, but Captain Swinfen was also conducting a war of attrition against her. He sent his friends to shoot over " his " estate with the connivance of Mr Bacon, tenant of one of the Swinfen farms, who had decided that it would suit his purpose better to throw in his lot with Captain Swinfen. But John Rock, Gamekeeper to the Swinfen estate, had other ideas. He arrested Farmer Bacon and the Captain's friends, and on the instructions of Patience they were brought before the magistrates of Lichfield as common poachers. It must have been with great satisfaction that Charles Simpson, as Clerk of the Peace, saw Thomas Bacon sentenced to a spell in Stafford Gaol and the others receive stiff fines. An unknown writer put the whole episode into verse in the form of a ballad, the original of which, in manuscript form is now among the Swinfen papers in the Staffordshire County Record Office.

A BALLAD

Dedicated to the Lady of The Manor of Swinfen

Dramatis Personae

Sad'un .... Heir at Law
Bad'un .... Farmer Bacon
Gammon .... Lawyer
Malice .... Mother of Sad'un & Leader of the Gang
Lady of The Manor
Rock Keeper to the Lady of The Manor

> Air " A Frog he would a wooing go "
> Old Bacon would a shooting go
>   Go ! . . . go ! . . . said Sad'un
> Whether his Lady would let him or no
> Oh ! Sad'un,, Bad'un, Gammon and Malice
>   Heigh ho ! says Bad'un

———

> So, off he set with his friends to shoot
>   Oh ! ho ! said Bad'un
> He hired some villains to beat and hoot
> Oh ! Sad'un, Bad'un, Gammon and Malice
>   Oh ! fie Bad'un !

But the Lady's bold Keeper was firm as a Rock
    Oh! oh! said Bad'un
And he boldly walked up to the pig-headed Block-
Head ... and said ... " Down with your gun "
  No go! ... Bad'un!

———

He coolly took up the game they had shot
    Heigh! ho! said Bad'un
And coolly he carried it off from the spot
    Heigh! ho! said Bad'un

———

And brave Rock was forced his Pheasants to kill
    Heigh ho! said Bad'un
That he had all reared with such trouble and skill
To keep them from Sad'un and Bad'un and Co
    Heigh ho! said Bad'un

———

The Lady then summoned old B to Court
    Oh! dear said Bad'un
The Magistrates soon put an end to his sport
    Oh! dear! said Bad'un

———

The old rogue now found that he'd been mistaken
    Heigh! ho! said Bad'un
And now I must think of " saving my Bacon "
    Heigh ho! said Bad'un

———

A rasher man Bacon could not well be
    Heigh ho! said Bad'un
From the frying pan, into the fire fell he
    And serve him right Bad'un

———

So here is an end of Bacon and fry
    Heigh ho! said Bad'un
In the foul beds they've made, there they must lie
    Sad'un, Bad'un and Mad'un

Succefs to the Lady of Swinfen's old Hall
    Ha! ha! Bad'un
Long, long may she live, may her Enemies fall
    Sad'un, Bad'un and Mad'un

———

January 19th 1857.

Another ballad on the same theme was printed and published as a broadsheet. The name of the author was not given, but on the copy deposited with some family papers at Stafford Record Office there is a pencilled note in Patience Swinfen's handwriting " Charles Simpson," so it a fair guess that he was responsible. The style of the ballad is in keeping with the political broadsheets published at election time in those days, a practice in which Simpson must have been well versed.

The reference in the third verse to " Williams, Willes and Crowder " is to three of the judges who heard the case in the Court of Common Pleas; " Fre-er " in verse four is a reference to Mr Frere, Captain Swinfen's attorney.

1857

THE SWINFEN BALLAD

There was a man of jaw,
    Named one Tummas Bacon,
He thought he knew the law,
    But he was mistaken.

Now this sporting peasant,
    He up and bought a gun,
For to pot a pheasant
    That was not his unn.

The Beaks they made him pay
    Smart for shot and powder,
The Lady wins the day
    With Williams Willes and Crowder.

The Captain now you see
    Is neither there nor here,
He made himself too Free
    And his dirty Lawyer Fre-er.

Quoth Tummas Bacon (chaw)
    " My neck is in a noose
" As game's agen the law
    " In course I cooks my goose."

So Tummas he mun go
    Straight to Stafford Prison,
For every one does so
    As prigs what is n't his'n.

This was not the only harassment carried out by Captain Swinfen (or, to be fair, more likely at the instigation of his mother, Mrs Francis Swinfen, " Malice " of the ballad and the " Leader of the Gang "). He persuaded some of the Swinfen tenants to withold their rents and as a result Patience lost £1,100 out of an annual income of £1,700. By this time she was only able to carry on " by the forebearance of the Lichfield tradesmen " as her counsel later put it. For by now the people of Lichfield had taken Patience's cause to their hearts and support and encouragement came from all sides and from all classes.

At this point there comes upon the scene the strange and tragic figure of Charles Rann Kennedy, scholar and Barrister at Law, who was to play a leading part in the fortunes of the Swinfen estates and in the life of Patience Swinfen.

Although of the same profession as Sir Frederick Thesiger, Kennedy was the complete opposite in character and temperament. He was born into an intellectual family, his brother being Dr Kennedy, Headmaster of Shrewsbury School and author of Kennedy's Latin Primer (known to countless schoolboys, including many still alive). The Kennedy family lived in Birmingham and Charles received his education at King Edward VI Grammar School, then, as now, renowned for its high scholastic standards.

From here he went as an exhibitioner to Trinity College Cambridge
in 1828, being elected Bell Scholar and winning the Porson Prize
two years running for Greek and Latin odes. After graduating B.A.
in 1831 he was elected a Fellow of his college, taking the degree
of M.A. in 1834. By this time he was reading law as a member of
Lincoln's Inn, and was called to the Bar in 1835.

In 1857, at the age of 49, he had a successful practice in the
Birmingham Circuit, living at Leamington with his wife and four
children.

He had followed with professional interest the case of the
Swinfen estate, and probably with some curiosity too, for in 1856
the idea of a member of the " weaker sex " fighting a lawsuit on
her own and standing up to seasoned members of the Bar was novel
indeed. He no doubt saw an opportunity for himself to achieve
that prominence in the legal world which had so far eluded him,
and he determined to make himself known to Mrs Swinfen as soon
as possible.

Normally a barrister is introduced to a client by the client's
solicitor (more often referred to in the time of the Swinfen case as
an attorney). But Charles Kennedy made no attempt to contact Mr
Simpson. Instead, he arranged the introduction on a social basis.
He had a cousin who lived at Shenstone, two or three miles from
Swinfen Hall. He invited himself over for a week and was able,
through a mutual aquaintance, Mrs Leisham, to secure an invitation
to the Hall. He expressed to Patience his admiration of her struggle
to maintain her rights and his wish to help her, and she quickly
responded to this offer of help. For all her determination and
courage she needed a man to lean on, and who better than Kennedy
to help her stand up to the might of the law? She invited him and
his family to come and stay at Swinfen, and he came with his four
children (but not Mrs Kennedy). They stayed for a fortnight, and
during that time Kennedy accepted the role of counsel to his
hostess and plans were made for the coming fight.

There is nothing like the sight of a beautiful woman in distress to stir the heart of a man, especially so when that woman has the warmth of character of the subject of this story. By the time he left Swinfen Hall, Charles Kennedy was hopelessly in love with Patience Swinfen and had appointed himself not only her counsel but also, in his own words, " her friend and protector." From then on they met and corresponded frequently and she addressed him in her letters as "My Dear Charles," signing herself "Yours affectionately" —not the usual method of communicating with one's legal representative.

In November 1857 the case came on before four Puisne Judges in the Court of Common Pleas, and Patience herself attended court ready, if necessary, to go to prison.   Kennedy presented her case with an eloquence and fervour that startled everybody.   The whole cause at the assize court was gone through in detail and it was shown that at no time had Mrs Swinfen ever consented to an agreement.   In fact, after her telegram of " offer refused " she had had no contact with her counsel, Sir Frederick Thesiger, whatever. Nor had she ever signed the written agreement which had been drawn up and in which the terms of agreement were stated.

The judges could do no other than accept the argument.   They ordered a re-trial of the original cause, to take place as before at Stafford Assizes.

Patience was jubilant, for now once again she had the chance to place her cause before a jury.   This time there would be no compromise, for on her orders Mr Simpson wrote this instruction into the brief, even though, once again, the counsel would be her dear Charles.

As for Charles, he was so elated that he published a booklet containing a report of the case, and on the first page he placed an ode which he had composed to his loved one.

TO PATIENCE SWINFEN

England hath need to thank thee, suffering Dame,
For thou shalt purge the volume of her laws
Of many an idle page of errors, flaws
By Ignorance traced, the record of her shame
Thine was a courage singly to exclaim
'Gainst Might perverting justice. For thy cause
Truth, Virtue, Wisdom stand. The glad applause
Of millions greets thee. Honoured be thy name!
The canting tones of dull Servility
In Halls of Themis shall be heard no more
And tricksters shall unlearn their crafty lore
So potent is thy spell! At sight of thee
Behold where Treason skulks with conscious dread
And base corruption hangs her guilty head.

One cannot help feeling that Anna Seward, the Swan of Lichfield, would have approved, but today one would expect something better from a Porson Prizewinner.

More down to earth were the five new verses which Charles Simpson composed for a second edition of his " Ballad of Swinfen."

Then " Well done," Pleader rare,
    Kennedy, Scholar ripe,
The bullies in their lair
    Shrieked at his iron gripe.

Bold, learned, keen and true,
    He dashed the flunkies down,
Westminster saw the crew
    Quailing beneath his frown.

Alone he stood—" Alone
    " But not dishonoured," He
Placed Justice on her throne,
    And shamed servility.

Then let us give nine cheers
For thee, true Lady fair,
Amid your smiles and tears
Our joy shall fill the air.

The British Flag unfurled
Waves o'er the brave and free,
For truth shall lick the world
With Pluck led on by Thee.

The re-trial at Stafford was fixed for 23rd July, 1858. Before it began a great deal of work was done by both Kennedy and Simpson. New witnesses were found who had seen Samuel Swinfen in the period shortly before his death, as, for example, Mr Barnes, his barber who came to shave him every Friday and had seen him only a few days before his death. At the age of eighty-one Barnes was able to make a very convincing testimony in the witness box which must have had considerable effect on the jury.

For the fortnight before the case opened Charles Kennedy came and stayed at Swinfen Hall while the final preparations were made.

By this time the case of Swinfen versus Swinfen had attracted national interest. In Lichfield it was the sole topic of conversation, and when it opened before Mr Justice Byles the court was crowded with friends from the city, including many ladies. Once again Charles Kennedy presented 'his client's case with tremendous eloquence and force. It was, in every aspect, the great moment of his life, with the attention of the general public as well as that of the members of his profession focused on him.

The outcome was in doubt right up to the end, the Judge being very non-commital in his summing-up and directions to the jury. When they retired the atmosphere in the court was electric, and only Patience appeared to be taking it calmly.

The jury were out for twenty minutes. There was a dramatic hush as they returned and as Mr Justice Byles asked the Foreman, "How do you find?" There was a pause, and then as he replied, "For the Plaintiff," tumultuous applause broke out in the court-room. It was some minutes before order could be restored. For Patience it must have been the most tremendous moment of her life. Not only was Swinfen now indisputably hers, but her honour had also been vindicated. In addition she felt that she had genuinely struck a blow for justice.

When the news reached Lichfield that evening they rang the bells of St Mary's Church for Patience Swinfen's victory, and crowds assembled in the streets to cheer her. The following day the bells of all the city churches rang throughout the day, and by midday a huge crowd had assembled at the old Trent Valley Station to meet the 12 o'clock train from Stafford. Patience was not on it, but the next train was at 4 o'clock, so the crowds waited, growing in size all the afternoon. At last the Stafford train pulled in, and as Patience Swinfen, their heroine, stepped from her carriage the crowds cheered and cheered and cheered again.

A procession formed up outside the station behind Mrs Swinfen's own carriage, and led by a military band they marched through Lichfield to the top of St John's Street. Every house between Trent Valley Station and Swinfen Hall was decorated with flags, flowers and laurels. The streets were lined with cheering crowds and all the church bells rang for joy. It was the hour of triumph for Patience Swinfen, one-time parlour maid and now the recognised mistress of Swinfen Hall, and also for the people of Lichfield who had made her cause their own.

Charles Kennedy shared in her triumph. Not only had he, as her knight in shining armour, slain the dragon for her, but he had triumphed over a legal injustice against which he had protested for years. But the strain of fighting the case had taken a toll of his health and for the next month he stayed at Swinfen Hall to recuperate. During this period he presented Patience with a ring containing a diamond flanked by two emeralds, and she vowed that as soon as she was able she would amply reward him for the exertions he had made on her behalf. Without him, she acknowledged, she would never have succeeded.

By now Patience must have had her fill of litigation, and would have been satisfied with what had been achieved. If the matter had been allowed to rest there, a great deal of money, time and unpleasantness would have been saved and she would have been able to enjoy the inheritance into which she had entered and the public esteem that she had earned. But Charles Kennedy had other ideas. Flushed with his triumph at Stafford Assizes he was now ready to carry his personal war against the legal system a step further. Sir Frederick Thesiger, the villain of the first trial, was now Lord Chelmsford and Lord Chancellor of England. To bring an action against him and win would be the crowning act in Kennedy's fight to achieve fame in his profession.

At first Patience was reluctant to proceed. She was not vindictive by nature, nor did she now need the money, but Kennedy was insistent and in the end she gave in. Proceedings were instituted to bring an action for damages against the Lord Chancellor. Mr Justice Cresswell, who had presided over the original hearing, was cited to appear as a witness. Kennedy, of course, would be counsel for the plaintiff, and it is difficult to imagine any situation in which a member of the Bar could achieve more notoriety in his profession.

The case of Swinfen versus Lord Chelmsford came on before a jury in the Court of Exchequer on 4th July 1859. Charles Kennedy in his opening speech made a bitter attack on Lord Chelmsord, but the case was doomed at the start. Dog does not eat dog, and it was hardly to be expected that the legal profession would acquiesce in the arraignment of one of their number for something which many of them had themselves done in their time. In his directions to the jury the judge pointed out that there was " agreement in fact " and " agreement in law." In vain did Charles Kennedy interrupt to question this legal fiction and ask what the Lord Chief Baron meant by " agreement in law." His question was brushed aside, and when the jury returned from their deliberations they announced a verdict in favour of Lord Chelmsford.

The general reaction to the verdict was summed up very well by the comments in the " *Illustrated London News* " (9th July 1859).

" Mrs Swinfen should have been satisfied with regaining her estate and should not have been induced to bring an action against her late counsel for assenting to a compromise. Mr Kennedy, her present counsel, should have conducted her case in a more becoming manner and not have caused everybody to rejoice in the defeat of a champion who evinced so much vulgarity. The Lord Chief Baron should not have endeavoured to affirm the semi-exploded proposition that a cousel should be entitled to decide whether a client should be entitled to fight out a case or not. On the other hand the three great legal witnesses, Lord Chelmsford, Sir Charles Cresswell and Sir (when is it to be Lord?) Alexander Cockburn acquitted themselves as might have been expected, and the jury very properly refused to give damages against the first for having exercised his judgment on a belief that the original cause was going against the lady, then his client. Mr Kennedy comes out of the matter worst, for he is a distinguished classical scholar whose *mores* have been left decidedly *feros* by studies usually held emollient."

The result of the case in the Court of Exchequer marks the downward turn in the fortunes of Charles Kennedy. He had antagonised the other members of his profession and he had lost his practice by neglect over the last three years during which he had spent all his time looking after the affairs of Patience. He removed to London where he tried to start a printing business at Sydenham, near the Crystal Palace. He and Patience still corresponded regularly; she worried about his health and was anxious if she did not hear from him for any length of time.

In the summer of 1860 she received a sudden and urgent summons from Charles to meet him in London the following day. She travelled up with her maid only and he met her at Euston Station and took them to lodgings which he had arranged nearby. Nothing was said except a request to meet him at a particular seat in the Zoological Gardens, Regents Park, the next morning.

They met and he told her that he was almost destitute and must have money, and he unfolded a scheme which he had prepared. It was, simply, that she should agree to a reversion of the Swinfen Estate in favour of Kennedy, so that on her death it would go to him. He hoped that when this had been signed, sealed and delivered he would be able to borrow at least £2,000 on the strength of it with which he could meet his immediate needs and provide capital for his business. When that had been done he would return the document to her. He reminded her of the debt she owed him and the promises of help she had made.

Patience went back to Swinfen without giving an answer. There was no one to whom she could turn for advice—Charles Simpson, her attorney would refuse to countenance the scheme, she felt sure, and there was no one else she could ask. In any case, Charles had insisted on secrecy.

She thought about it for some days and then wrote to him agreeing. They met several days later at an attorney's office in Birmingham and he produced the indenture which he himself had drawn up. At this time Charles Kennedy was 52 and Patience Swinfen was 47, so she had a greater expectation of life than him. But in the deed she was described as " aged 53." She duly signed, and at his request also signed a will in his favour.

A few day later she wrote to him, " I told you in one of my letters, five weeks ago, that I would die were it necessary to save you. You probably thought these vain words. Such a sacrifice is not required, but what was required I have cheerfully done for you, and a thousand times more would I do for you if I had the power."

But unfortunately for Kennedy the scheme turned out to be in vain. He found he was unable to borrow anything on the reversion, and soon he was pleading with Patience for financial help again. She gave him £200, which with the brief fees he had already received made up a total of £905. It was all she could do without mortgaging or selling part of the estate, which she was now reluctant to do.

Matters came to a head in the autumn of 1861. She had gone, in October, to stay with some friends, the Reids, at their home at Berridale, Dumbartonshire. While there she met a friend of the Reids, Charles Wilsone Broun of Linnburn, a little village on the eastern side of the Gareloch. He was a widower with two daughters of eight and nine and two little boys of seven and four. Before she returned to Swinfen he had proposed to Patience and she had accepted him. She wrote to Charles Kennedy returning his ring and explaining what had happened. " I know how you must feel," she wrote, "but you cannot imagine how lonely it is for me without anyone. You have your wife and children."

At first Kennedy was, in his own words, " nearly insane." But his feelings soon turned to anger and rage. Hell, it is said, has no fury like a woman scorned, but the same can apply to some men. He wrote to all Patience's friends; the Rowleys, the Rev. Cowpland, Charles Simpson and any others he knew of, informing them of his intention to publish a pamphlet entitled " The Serpent of Swinfen " in which he would show how he had been tricked by Patience. It would consist of extracts from her letters to him, and he immediately got to work on it and arranged for a printing of 250 copies. At the same time he set in motion an action against Patience for £20,000 which he claimed as the costs he had incurred on her behalf.

In the meantime Patience and Charles Broun had been married quietly at Weeford Parish Church by the Reverend Robert Cowpland, by licence, on the 17th December, 1861. Charles and Caroline Swinfen were the witnesses. Charles Broun brought his children to Swinfen, which became their home, and he and his wife adopted the surname of Swinfen-Broun.

By now Patience must have been weary of the law and only too anxious to forget it and start her new life. But once again she had to go through the whole sorry business at Warwick assizes. Kennedy made the most of the opportunity to have his revenge on her and all the details of their friendship were brought out in court, even to the use of her letters to him in evidence. What, one wonders, did his own family feel about it? He won his case and was awarded the full amount of £20,000.

But by now Charles Broun was involved, and he took the case to the court of Common Pleas. There the situation was reversed, on the grounds that a barrister cannot sue for his fees, for he receives, by custom, no fees—only honoraria.

It was the last act in a long drawn out drama. By now Kennedy was a sick and despirited man, and there was no fight left in him. He died four years later, at the age of 59.

*   *   *

At last after eight years of courts and litigation, Patience Swinfen-Broun was able to enjoy her inheritance and bring up her step-children at Swinfen Hall. Before she died in 1876, the little boy, Michael Alexander Swinfen-Broun had begun his career in the army, with the South Staffordshire Regiment. On the death of his father in 1883 he succeeded to the Swinfen Estate and lived there for the next sixty-five years.

Colonel Swinfen-Broun and his wife Laura are remembered today as two of the most generous benefactors that the City of Lichfield has ever known. To them we owe Beacon Park, part of which was given at the request of Mrs Swinfen-Broun after her death in 1932, and the remainder left by Colonel Swinfen-Broun on his death in 1948. He also founded the Swinfen-Broun Trust which has given financial help to many institutions in the city ever since—one of the latest examples of its work being the furnishing of the Swinfen-Broun Suite in the Civic Hall. In the field of sport, in their work for the Victoria Hospital and in their many gifts of silver to the civic plate, they are still remembered today.

By one of those ironies or fate which sometimes occur, the legal system, which Patience Swinfen had fought so courageously and successully, in her bid for the Swinfen Estate, had the last word. On the death of Colonel Swinfen-Broun in 1948 the estate was sold and purchased by the Crown. Today Swinfen Hall is one of Her Majesty's Prisons, and the house itself is silent and empty.

CHAPTER IX

High Victorian Gothic
Sir Gilbert Scott at Lichfield

During the 18th century the life of the Church of England had
reached a very low ebb. We have already seen the state into which
Lichfield Cathedral had sunk, and a similar attitude prevailed in
the parish churches. As an example of this, St Chad's Church
was fairly typical, not only of church life in Lichfield, but of the
country in general. At the beginning of the 19th century there was
only one service on Sunday, this being Morning Prayer, and
Communion was celebrated only four times in the year. But the
best indication of the religious philosophy of the time can be gained
from a study of pictures of the interior of the church at this time.

Over the chancel arch, in a prominent position, the Royal Coat
of Arms was displayed, symbolising the subserviance of the Church
to the State. Below it stood a three-decker pulpit, the most
prominent article of furniture in the building, and obviously the
focal point of worship. In contrast, the altar (or Holy Table as it
would then be described) occupied an inconspicuous position in
the chancel, out of sight of most of the congregation. A plain,
refectory-type table, bearing the date 1667, it had none of the
furnishings that it has today, and was accorded little reverence.
Indeed, it might well, as was the case in many other churches, have
been used by the congregation as a depository for their hats and
coats. Most certainly it would be used as a convenient place on
which to enter up the register after baptisms, deaths and marriages,
as faded ink-stains show to this day.

In the three-decker pulpit the Parish Clerk occupied the lowest deck, from which position he intoned the psalms and responses. (Only cathedral choirs sang the offices of the church, and not very well at that). In the middle deck sat the parson in a white surplice, which he doffed at sermon time and replaced with a black gown, before ascending to the top deck to deliver his sermon. From here he would look down on his congregation seated in their high box-pews, each pew appropriated to a particular person or family, who paid a " pew rent " for this privilege and who were shown to their pew before the service by an old lady who acted as " pew-opener." She also ensured that no unauthorised persons gate-crashed into a pew. For paupers and such as could not afford a pew rent there were benches placed along the length of the centre aisle.

At the back of the church, facing the parson in his pulpit, and at about the same height, was a gallery. Here sat the children and the choir, the latter a group of men and women dressed in their ordinary clothes. They led the singing of the hymns, probably from a Tate & Brady hymnal, and were sometimes accompanied by a string and wind band. Nothing more ambitious than this was ever attempted.

Such was a typical parish church in the 1830s. But perhaps the most surprising thing of all, as one looks around the interior, is the complete lack of any sign or symbol that might identify it as a place of Christian worship. Even the memorials on the walls, while testifying in somewhat extravagent terms to the lives of the departed while on earth, make not the slightest reference to any hopes concerning their future state. The atmosphere is thoroughly pagan, in keeping with the philosophy of the Age of Reason.

Things were about to change, however, and the change came about as a result of two movements which originated in the universities of Oxford and Cambridge. The Oxford Movement, or the Tractarian Movement as it is sometimes called, is usually considered to have begun with the Assize sermon preached by John Keble at Oxford in July 1833. Keble (1792 to 1866) was a Fellow of Oriel, ordained in 1816 and Professor of Poetry at Oxford from

1831 to 1841. His fellow-tractarians were Richard Hurrell Froude, Edward Bouverie Pusey, and best-known to all, John Henry Newman, who later was to join the Roman Catholic Church.

Between them they published, in the years between 1833 and 1841, no less than 90 " Tracts for the Times " in which they called for a " Via Media " between the superstitions of the Church of Rome on the one hand and the errors of Protestantism on the other. They stressed the Catholic and Apostolic nature of the Church of England, pointed out that the Book of Common Prayer had its origins in pre-Reformation liturgies and emphasised the importance of the regular and reverent administration of the sacraments. And in all this they sought to raise the standard of church worship from the slovenly and irreverent level to which it had fallen.

The Oxford Movement was essentially intellectual, but at Cambridge its counterpart, the Camden Society (named after the historian) took a more practical view. Their aim was to restore the right setting for worship through the media of architecture, church furnishings and music. Their views were published through a periodical, *The Ecclesiologist,* which had a tremendous influence on the clergy, on churchmen and particularly on architects. The Camden Society believed, with Pugin, that Gothic was the only true kind of Christian architecture, and for England that meant Early English, Decorated or Perpendicular. From then on, throughout the 19th century and well into the 20th, almost every church that was built, or every old church that was rebuilt was conceived in one of these styles. Sometimes they incorporated more than one style—whether from ignorance or the desire to produce a false appearance of archaeological growth is not always clear.

One of the earliest architects to follow the teaching of the Camden Society was Thomas Johnson of Lichfield who, as already mentioned, designed quite a number of churches in Staffordshire. His earliest example of Camdenism is at St Michael's, Lichfield, which he rebuilt in 1842, but his finest example is All Saints, Leigh. This church was rebuilt in 1846 at the cost of Lord Bagot of Blithfield and is exceptional for a village church, consisting of a crossing tower, chancel of three bays with superb stone rib-vaulting, transepts of two bays and a five-bay nave. The style is Decorated, carried out with impeccable accuracy and fully in accordance with the tenets of the Camdenians.

The Camden Society were also concerned very much with the furnishing of the church and their use. The old three-decker pulpits were swept away; so too were the Royal Coats of Arms.* The altar once again became the focal point of worship, the wooden communion table being sometimes replaced by that abomination of all true Protestants, a stone altar. Congregations were relegated to the nave, and the box pews in the choir were replaced by choir stalls, occupied now by a surpliced choir. At first there was little music for them to sing, but that, as we shall see, was soon taken care of.

The combined pattern of worship set by the Oxford Movement and the Camden Society has influenced the practice of the Anglican Church ever since. But along with new ways went also a new order and reverence that had been lacking before.

In propagating these ideas, two men from Lichfield were to play very important roles. The first of these was Frederick Oakley, author of the universally-known Christmas hymn, Adeste Fidelis (O come All Ye Faithful). Oakley was the sixth son of Sir Charles Oakley, who had retired from a Governorship in India to Lichfield, where he resided in the Bishop's Palace. (The Palace, it should be explained, although built in 1687, was never inhabited by a Bishop of Lichfield until about 1860. Before that, Bishops resided at Eccleshall). Frederick Oakley was something of a musical prodigy, and at the age of eight was allowed to accompany the psalms on the cathedral organ for weekday services. He went up to Oxford in the 1830s and became immersed in the Tractarian movement. He took Holy Orders and in 1839 came to London as Priest-in-Charge of Margaret Chapel, Margaret Street, Marylebone.

---

* Such is the perversity of human nature that the few of these relics of the past that still exist are now cherished for their scarcity value. St Michael's, Lichfield still has a fine example of the Royal Coat of Arms of Queen Anne (of Queen Anne's Bounty fame).

It was a small, unpretentious chapel with a previous history as a conventicle. It consisted of one large room with a low, flat, whitewashed ceiling and a large, central three-decker pulpit. This Oakley removed at the first opportunity and re-established the altar as the focal point of the church. On it he placed candlesticks, an alms-dish, a bible and flowers at festivals. He recruited local boys to form a choir and clothed them in surplices and then, as there was no musical setting of the Anglican liturgy for them to sing he co-operated with his organist in producing the first Anglican Gregorian psalter, *Laudes Diurnae*. He held daily services and observed the regular cycle of Saints' Days, seasons, fasts and feasts. Soon Margaret Chapel became well-known nationally, attracting growing congregations. Almost every clergyman visiting London called in at Margaret Street to see what was going on, whether to criticise or approve. Many prominent men of the day worshipped there, including William Ewart Gladstone who later wrote that the services there were the most devotional he had ever attended.

But this was not achieved without great difficulty. The Bishop of London received constant complaints from extreme Protestants who railed at Oakley's " ritualistic practices." With most of these the Bishop sympathised and issued various episcopal sanctions. Finally, in 1845, he had Oakley arraigned before the Court of Arches, the highest ecclesiastical court in the land. He was charged with publishing one or more tracts containing expressions which raised doubts as to his adherance to the Thirty Nine Articles. To these allegations he did not plead, and the judge, Sir Herbert Jenner Fust, after a very elaborate judgment, revoked Oakley's licence as Minister of the Margaret Chapel. He also ordered that the judgment should be read on the following Sunday in the chapel.

The following Sunday Margaret Chapel was crowded. Expectant crowds waited to see what would happen. The assistant priest, the Reverend W. Richardson, officiated and no mention of the judgment was made. Frederick Oakley never appeared, and later it was announced that he had been accepted into the Church of Rome. It was a path that many other Tractarians were to follow in the years to come. Although Oakley's incumbency of the Margaret Street Chapel was only six years, the work he did there made an indelible impression on the Anglican Church. Today his church, rebuilt as All Saints, Margaret Street is known all over the world as a centre of Anglo-Catholicism.

The other person we must note is the Reverend Thomas Helmore. Born in 1811, he was the son of a Congregationalist minister and like Frederick Oakeley he was an accomplished musician. In 1837 he went up to Oxford where the Tractarian Movement was just getting into its stride, and, again like Oakley, when Helmore graduated B.A. in 1840 he decided to take orders. He was ordained Deacon and Priest by special dispensation in the same year and his first appointment was as curate of St Michael's Church, Lichfield. St Michael's, it will be remembered, was one of the first churches to be rebuilt in the style advocated by the Ecclesiologist, in 1842, shortly after Helmore had arrived there. It is interesting to surmise how much his advice entered into the architect's plans.

Shortly afterwards he was appointed Priest-Vicar at Lichfield Cathedral where his duties consisted of intoning the services and singing with the choir. He developed an interest in Gregorian chanting, which led him to become a member of the Motet Society. Through this connection he made the acquaintance of Mr (later Sir) Thomas Dyke Acland, a prominent churchman and a governor of St Marks College, Chelsea. St Mark's was one of the new Church of England training colleges for teachers, formed to meet the growing demand as new schools began to spring up all over the country. From the start it had a strong musical tradition; in the college chapel a fully choral service was sung daily by a choir consisting of members of the student body together with trebles drawn from the pupils of the " Model School " in the grounds of the college where the students practiced their teaching.

Through Mr Acland's recommendation Thomas Helmore was appointed to the post of Principal at St Mark's late in 1842. He realised the full implications of the work he was taking on, for he would be shaping the future form of liturgical worship in the Anglican Church. His students would be going as teachers to schools all over the country; parochial schools attached to particular churches, and they would be expected to help in the setting up and training of the new style of church choir that was coming into being as a result of the revival in church worship started by the Tractarians.   He determined that they should be given an example to work by of the very highest standard, and before long the choral services of St Mark's College were attracting congregations from all over London, just as Oakley's had done at Margaret Street.   After five years hard work Helmore was able to say that his choir was able to sing " ten entire cathedral services, by Tallis, Farrant, Byrd, Gibbons, Bevin, Batten, Chreyghton, Rogers, Aldridge and Boyce, with two other morning services by Bancroft and Travers, a Communion service adapted from Victoria and another from Palestrina."   In addition over seventy anthems were in general use.   When the Model School was in session Anglican plainsong chants were used, but during the school holidays, when the choir was without trebles, the Gregorian mode was employed, this being Helmore's own special study.

All this was a far cry from the barrel-organ and Tate & Brady Hymnal of the early 19th century parish churches, and represented an impossibly high standard for most parochial choirs.   It did mean however, that teachers with a thorough knowledge of what was possible were able to take that knowledge with them wherever they went.   It shaped the pattern of worship in Anglican churches for the next hundred years.   In doing so it naturally incurred the wrath of the Evangelicals, but fortunately Helmore escaped the fate of Oakley and went on to become Master of the Choristers of the Chapels Royal.   Among those who passed through his hands was young Arthur Sullivan, who freely admitted in later years that it was the teaching and encouragement of Helmore that enabled him to win the Mendlessohn Scholarship that took him to Leipzig in 1857.   So perhaps it can be said that it is due to the work of a former curate of St Michael's Church, Lichfield that we owe the immortal works of Gilbert and Sullivan.

One effect of the 19th century revival in church life was a tremendous building and rebuilding of churches.   About one third of the parish churches in England today were built at this time, mostly in the new industrial towns which had sprung up or expanded.   In addition almost every existing church was "restored" to a greater or lesser extent, and all this was done in the spirit of the Camden Society as expounded in the "Ecclesiologist"; a movement which led eventually to what became known as "High Victorian Gothic." One of the chief exponents of this was Mr (later Sir) Gilbert Scott, who, it will be remembered, had visited Lichfield in the 1840s to build the Union Workhouse.

In 1856 he returned to the city at the invitation of the Dean and Chapter to take charge of a complete restoration of the cathedral, a restoration which was carried out for the next forty years. So complete was this work that a stranger to the building might be forgiven for assuming that Scott had created an entirely new edifice, and he has been much criticised ever since for being too drastic. Before accepting such criticism, however, it is as well to consider what the state of the cathedral was when he came to it. Canon Lonsdale (Vicar of St Mary's, 1866-1879) has left a revealing description in his "Recollections."

"The nave and transepts," he writes, "were absolutely empty of furniture of any kind, except that the south transept contained the fittings of the Dean's Consistory Court (since abolished), and in the north transept, where the organ now is,* stood the statue of Bishop Ryder, raised on a high pedestal and looking as if it were about to tumble forward. The walls, arches and pillars were one uniform, dead, yellowish whitewash, many coats thick; as also the choir from end to end and from top to bottom, and indeed the whole interior. The nave was quite unused; indeed, except during service hours the Verger's Silver Key alone gave admission to any part of the church. The two parts of the building were entirely separate from each other. The choir was entered by a door under a high partition, composed of remains of the original High Altar, fourteenth century screen and of other materials. This partition filled the whole of the first bay of the present choir. On either side of the entrance were vestries for the Lay Vicars and the Choristers, and above this was placed the organ; the rest of the space up to the roof being filled in with glass, so that the separation of the nave and choir was complete.

---

* i.e., until 1908, when it was removed to its present position.

In the choir itself the remains of the reredos, which stood at the spot where the present one is now fixed, had been removed by Wyatt at the end of the last century,* and the Holy Table was carried to the extreme end of the Lady Chapel. On either side, from the screen up to the very entrance to the Lady Chapel, were pews made of oak lined with green baize and studded with brass nails. The choir aisles on either side were entirely shut out from the choir, the arches being filled in with plaster, in order, as it was imagined, to help towards warmth. In the three bays eastward from the screen—the second, third and fourth as they are now—stalls were fixed, composed of plaster, wood, rope, nails and much else, with canopies of the same material over them, which the old Verger of that day used to call ‘ beautiful tabernacle work.’ The Dean and Canons Residentiary had stalls facing eastward in the screen under the organ. The choir aisles, shut out from the choir, were long narrow passages, never used, ending on the north side in a blank wall, and on the south side with the monument of the ‘ Sleeping Children ’.”

Such was the inside of the cathedral, and these facts must be borne in mind when passing judgment on Sir Gilbert Scott.

Apart from the clearing away of the excresences mentioned above, the opening up of the arches and the replacement of mouldings and carved stonework which had been removed or mutliated before the application of the ubiquitous Roman cement, Scott also furnished new and original work. The principal examples of this are the choir and prebendal stalls, the High Altar and reredos, the metalwork gates and choir screen and the pulpit. The gates, the choir screen and the pulpit were all designed by Scott and carried out by Skidmore of Coventry. The screen is a very highly-ornamented structure in wrought-iron, copper and brass, the first of four similar ones, the other three being at Worcester, Hereford and Salisbury cathedrals. Like so many forms of Victorian art, they depend on the brilliance of the metals and of the colours for their effect, and in recent times the effect of one hundred years of gaslight, coke fumes and general air pollution had

---

* i.e., the 18th century.

sadly tarnished their appearance. The answer to this at Salisbury and Hereford was to demolish and scrap; at Lichfield it was to clean and refurbish so that it is now in its original state, effecting a startling transformation. Comparison with the pulpit still awaiting cleaning, makes a most interesting comparison of " before and after."

The work of restoring the interior was completed in five years, and the re-opening was marked by a day of celebration on 22nd October 1861. Many thousands of people attended the services on that day; there were eight hundred communicants and six hundred clergy, and the principal service, conducted by the Rev. Thomas Helmore, Master of the Choir of Her Majesty's Chapels Royal, was sung by nine hundred and fifty members of choirs from all over the Diocese. For Helmore, that alone must have been one of the greatest tributes that had ever been paid to the work that he had done for the advancement of choral worship in the Church, and the culmination of his labours at St. Mark's.

Bishop Wilberforce preached the sermon, and the collection amounted to £700.

Following the restoration of the interior, work began on the outside of the cathedral, and in 1877 Sir Gilbert Scott turned his attention to the West Front. Here again he has often been accused of a too-thorough restoration, so it is as well to consider the problem that confronted him.

The original state of the West Front in mediaeval times has already been described in Chapter I. By the 18th century time and the destruction wrought by the Puritans during the Civil War had played havoc with the beautiful tracery and statuary. All those statues within reach of the pikes and halberds of the soldiers were smashed and pulled down; those higher up were damaged by musket shot. During the following century, in 1749, those statues which remained were taken down on the orders of a Dean who fancied that the figures nodded to him as he entered the church. The only exceptions to this were five figures at the very top of the eastern side of the north-west tower.

In 1820 the whole of the West Front, reported at that time to be in a very dilapidated state, was covered with Roman cement. What this involved can be gathered from the following account, in the "*Gentleman's Magazine*," in 1824.

"Surely everyone must lament the manner in which the West Front . . . has lately been restored. The whole of the beautiful facade is now of plaster, appearing with all its original ornaments— at least, a resemblance of them—excepting the statues, the greater number of which, having been utterly destroyed, can never be replaced.

The operation a structure must go through before it is coated with this detestable substance is more destructive to its appearance than the united injuries of time and violence for many centuries. The West Front, already roughened by antiquity, was hatched and chipped till it resembled a huge rock on which we could here and there discover a feature that seemed to proclaim the fabric a work of art. Thus prepared, the walls were plastered and the arches and ornaments formed, in some instances according to ancient authority, and in others according to the judgment of the plasterers . . .

Lichfield Cathedral is an ill-fated building. It was sadly dilapidated in the 17th century and again mangled by Wyatt, and it is to be feared that very little of the ancient work will remain untouched on the exterior."

Faced with a restoration of such magnitude, Sir Gilbert Scott's first action was to remove the statues, cast in Roman cement, which had been placed along the bottom stage of the West Front in 1820, at the same time that the Front was covered with stucco. They were the work of a Mr Joseph Harris, of Bath, from drawings of the statues at Wells Cathedral, made by Joseph Potter Jnr., and so were in no way replicas of what had been there originally. Two or three of them can still be seen in the upper part of the crossing tower, where they were stored in 1877. The standard of artistic achievement reached by Mr Harris can be likened to that of the concrete gnomes produced today for use as garden ornaments.

Next, the layer of Roman cement was removed, laying bare the " hatching and chipping " referred to by the " *Gentleman's Magazine.*" As practically all traces of the original moulding and ornament had been removed, Scott had to re-design the carving that was to be applied to the new surface. To guide him in this he had a small amount of detail work as well as the five original statues, all on the uppermost stage of the north-west tower where they had escaped not only the ravages of time, but also the incrustations of Roman cement. From these few remains, and by studying pictures of the cathedral from the past, every effort was made to ensure as faithful a reproduction as possible of the original work.

Two methods of applying the carving could be used—the application of a thin ashlar, which would then be carved, or by cutting back into the existing stone work for the required distance. Scott chose the second of these alternatives. The result is a completely new West Front to the design of Sir Gilbert Scott. It is difficult, however, to see what else he could have done. In the process of restoration the opportunity was taken to place new statues (this time carved in stone) in the niches. The large statue of King Charles II, at the top of the central gable, was removed and replaced by the more appropriate figure of Christ in Glory, the work of a London sculptress, Miss Grant. King Charles was banished to the inside of the north-west tower, where he remained for some ninety years. He is now re-sited outside the cathedral, by the south door.

The smaller statues were given by various donors over several years. The majority were the work of Mr Robert Bridgeman, founder of the Lichfield firm of ecclesiastical craftsmen who now carry out work for churches all over the world, and who still care for the fabric of the cathedral today. Other statues were the work of Miss Grant, already mentioned, and of a Mr Seale of Brixton. Miss Grant was not the only sculptress to work on the restoration of the West Front, for among the figures is one of Queen Victoria, the reigning monarch.* It was the work of her daughter, the Princess Louise, another example of whose work, also a statue of her mother, can be seen in Kensington Gardens.

---

* Third from the left, on the third row down.

Most visitors regard the figures on the West Front as a whole, and the effect is, without doubt, an impressive one. But a study of the individual figures (and for the higher ones this requires binoculars) is well worth the effort; here one will find, as well as the Angels and Archangels, Patriarchs and Prophets, such diverse characters as King Alfred with his harp (at one time confused with King David), King Wulfere with a model of the Saxon cathedral in his hand, Bishop Clinton with a model of the Norman one at his feet, and Bishop Langton with a model of the Lady Chapel, of which he was the builder.

The restoration of the West Front was completed in 1881, and dedicated by the Archbishop of Canterbury on 29th May, 1884. With it the restoration begun by Scott in 1856 was completed, inasmuch as any restoration of a building such as Lichfield Cathedral can be said to be complete. He had set out to make it, as near as possible, a building such as it had been on its completion in the 14th century. How far he succeeded it is difficult to say, but it is certain that the condition in which he left it was incomparably better than that in which he found it.

The total cost of the work had amounted to £82,000.

CHAPTER X

Lichfield Elections

From the year 1304 until 1868, the city of Lichfield returned two members to Parliament. In the hundred years before 1865 both members were the nominees of the Anson and Leveson Gower families, representing the Whig, and later the Liberal interests. So strong was the influence of these two families in Lichfield, where they owned considerable property, that no Tory candidate had any hope of success; for a period of thirty-eight years the two seats were never contested.

In 1834, however, a Tory champion appeared on the scene in the person of Captain Richard Dyott, eldest son of General William Dyott of Freeford. He was nominated by no less a person than the great Sir Robert Peel, then living at Drayton Manor. Richard Dyott was still in his early twenties, and his youthful appearance was the subject of a comment from one of the Wrottesleys, another local Whig family, who asked Sir Robert what he intended to do with him. " Make a Junior Lord of the Treasury of him, if he isn't fit for anything else," was the retort. (The Wrottesley in question occupied that position).

Captain Dyott was unsuccessful on that occasion, but in 1841, in the election that followed the dissolution of Lord Melbourne's ministry, he came very near to winning a seat, being defeated by only eight votes. This, of course, was not nearly so close as it would be today, since the total electorate of Lichfield at that time was less than 900. This figure represented quite a small part of the male population; the bailiffs, magistrates, 40 shilling free-holders, burgage tenants and enrolled freemen paying scot and lot (rates). This last group, the freemen of the City Companies were by far the largest group, consisting of 420 members. They belonged

to seven Companies, the successors to the ancient mediaeval guilds,
formed originally to control the admission to and the conditions of
work in particular trades.   In 1841 the Lichfield Companies consisted of the Butchers and Chandlers; Bakers; Corvisers and
Curriers; Dyers, Weavers and Clothworkers; Saddlers, Glovers,
Whittawers and Bridle Cutters; Tailors; Smiths, Goldsmiths, Card
Makers, Ironmongers, Plumbers, Braziers, Pewterers, Nailors and
Spurriers.   Freemen of these companies had to reside within seven
miles of the centre of the city, and were admitted to the Company
in one of three ways—birth, servitude or compounding.   Birth gave
the right of admission to the eldest sons of Freemen; servitude gave
it to those who had served an apprenticeship with a Freeman, and
compounding allowed a person who had served an apprenticeship
elsewhere than in Lichfield to be admitted on payment of a sum
of money (at this time £10).   Originally all these Freemen had the
right to vote at Parliamentary elections, but the Reform Act of
1832 disenfranchised the compounders.   The same act also vested
the power of admitting Freemen in the Mayor of the Borough, who
was required to examine the claims of a new entrant, and on these
being established to have his name enrolled by the Town Clerk, in
a book authorised for that purpose by the Act, called the Roll of
Freemen, a copy of which was to be at all times open to the
inspection of the Burgesses.

Elections took place over a period of eight or nine days, the
state of the poll being announced daily at four o'clock in the afternoon.   Voting took place on the hustings, a covered platform
erected in the Market Place.   Here, on the opening day, the
candidates were nominated, and thereafter electors made their
choice.   This was done verbally to the Polling Clerk, in full view
of the general public. so that there was no chance of keeping one's
views secret.   A voter who went against the wishes of his landlord
or employer could be pretty certain of the word getting back to
them, and his tenancy or his job might be in jeopardy.

The nine days of the election was rather like an extended
Bower Day, with church bells ringing, bands parading the streets
and a general feeling of excitement in the air.   The bands headed
processions in which the candidates were carried shoulder-high

in chairs which were specially made for the purpose, gilded and dressed and fitted with carrying poles. As many as eighteen dressers and twenty-six chair carriers might be employed, and the Lichfield Morris Men would also be engaged to take part in the procession. Ale and spirits flowed freely at the public houses, and fights were not uncommon, as, for example, when two rival processions met in the streets. In 1826 the George Hotel, headquarters of the Whigs, had all its windows smashed and the Militia had to be sent for from Birmingham to restore order. Elections were enjoyed by the majority of the population as an opportunity for making some extra money, for drinking at someone else's expense and for the excitement of all the goings-on, especially the chance of watching or taking part in a good punch-up.

In view of the closeness of the 1841 election result it was decided by Captain Dyott and his party that they would appeal. A petition was accordingly lodged. A contemporary account of this fact stated " In February 1842, the newspapers gave a list of all the election petitions throughout the country, with various letters of the alphabet denoting the different grounds—such as T for treating, &c. Lichfield was prominent in the list, having every possible letter against it except R for riot." *

The date of the appeal was fixed for 22nd April, 1842. The hearing took place in Lichfield Guildhall before a panel of seven M.P's, Mr Divett, M.P. for Exeter, being in the Chair. If today this seems to us rather like the members of a club conferring on whether to admit a new member, let us not forget that the House of Commons has on many occasions been referred to as the best club in Britain.

Mr Austin Q.C. opened the case on behalf of the Petitioner, Captain Dyott. He based his case on the fact that, firstly, seven freemen of the city, who would have voted for Dyott, had applied to the Mayor to be examined for admission to the Roll of Freemen but this had not been done, and consequently they were unable to

---

* " The Lichfield Election Petition " by " Anti-Bubble."
James Meacham, Printer, Lichfield, 1842.

cast their votes. The significance of this point was that both the Mayor, and also the Town Clerk, Mr Charles Simpson, were supporters of the opposite party.

In addition, alleged Mr Austin, there had been personations of voters who did not cast their votes, cases of persons who received alms to induce them to vote, and in particular what he described as " influence of a singular description." Lord Lichfield (whose son, Sir George Anson, had been one of the successful candidates) had been Postmaster-General in the last administration. While in that position, asserted Mr Austin, " he was enabled to confer favours in the shape of offices in the Post Office Department on various inhabitants of Lichfield. And in the course of the last two years it does appear, that such is the pre-eminent capacity of persons born and living in Lichfield, and particularly that class who are entitled to be freemen in Lichfield, and are entitled to vote there, or their relations; such is their pre-eminent capacity for transacting Post Office business, that it has been found expedient to appoint no less than fifty of such individuals to the Post Office in London and the Post Office Department in Liverpool."

In his reply Mr Hill Q.C., counsel for the sitting member, Lord Alfred Paget, denied the various allegations and as far as the matter of the Post Office appointments were concerned said that the people of Lichfield should be grateful to Lord Lichfield for providing such opportunities for employment !

The various witnesses were then examined and cross-examined, a great deal of information of a personal nature emerging as a result which must have provided much satisfactory gossip in the city for a week at least—information as to people's drinking habits, as to who lived where and with whom, as to who owned particular properties and the like—matters which have always been, and still are, of great importance in a small city such as Lichfield.

In due course the Committee retired to consider their decision. They returned to announce that they upheld the election of Lord Alfred Paget.

Lord Alfred, in conjunction with various members of the Anson family, represented Lichfield for the next 24 years. During this time Captain " Dick " Dyott (as he was universally known in and around the city) continued to nurse the constituency for the Tories. In the election of 1859, which led to Lord Palmerstone's ministry, Captain Dyott's old friend and business associate, Richard Croft Chawner, was a Tory candidate but was unsuccessful. It was on this occasion that Charles Rann Kennedy, fresh from his triumph at Stafford Assizes, wrote to Patience Swinfen to ask about the possibility of his standing for Lichfield. Her reply was not encouraging and he did not pursue it further.

The Liberals had it all their own way until 1865, when Colonel Richard Dyott, as he now was, resolved to enter the lists once more. His two Liberal opponents were Major Augustus Anson V.C.,* and Lord Alfred Paget. The result of a hard-fought contest was: Major Anson, 302 votes; Colonel Dyott; 257 votes; Lord Alfred Paget 209 votes. At last, after 33 years and three attempts Dick Dyott had realised his ambition of a seat in the House.

Three years later, after the Representation of the People Act of 1867 had reduced Lichfield's representation to one M.P., there was a straightforward fight between Colonel Dyott and Major Anson, and Dyott was the victor. The extension of the franchise had done away with the influence which the Anson family had held for so long. The Liberals did not give up without a fight, however, and a petition was lodged against Colonel Dyott's return.

It is interesting to compare the trial of this petition with the one held in 1842. No longer was the hearing carried out by a panel of M.P's, but now it was a judicial inquiry, done with all the solemnity of a court of law. Here is how the Staffordshire Advertiser of 28th January, 1869, described it.

---

* Major Anson had a distinguished military career, being one of the earliest winners of the Victoria Cross. He instituted the Anson Sword at the Royal Military College, Sandhurst, to be awarded annually, by permission of Her Majesty Queen Victoria, to the best cadet of the year.

" The trial of the petition presented by Major the Hon. Augustus Henry Archibald Anson V.C., against the return of Col. Richard Dyott, M.P., as member for Lichfield, began on Tuesday before the Hon. Mr Justice Willes,* one of the three judges appointed for the trial of election petitions in England. Mr Justice Willes arrived at the Trent Valley station from London by the 1.43 p.m. train, and was met by the Mayor's carriage, in which he was conveyed to his lodgings, a handsome residence in St John Street, which Capt. Webster, the occupant, had temporarily vacated. At half-past three a procession, headed by the Mayor, R. Crosskey Esq., the Sheriff, Mr F. Williams, and accompanied by the City Police, under the superintendence of Chief Constable Mynard, a few of the Birmingham police, and the Corporation officials, carrying the Mace etc., proceeded to the Judge's lodgings. There they were joined by his Lordship, who, riding in the Mayor's carriage, was conducted in state to the Guildhall. A large crowd awaited the arrival of the procession. On the Judge taking his seat on the bench the court was speedily filled. The arrangements for preventing confusion in court were very efficient, and convenient accommodation was provided for counsel, witnesses and reporters. Col. Dyott M.P. and Major Anson occupied seats within the bar, next to their learned counsel.

Shortly after four o'clock the Court was formally opened by the Judge's Clerk calling on the case of ' City of Lichfield Election Petition. Anson against Dyott.'

Mr James Montgomery was then sworn in as shorthand writer. The evidence was gone through much more expeditiously than is usual at Assizes, the Judge taking brief notes only, and when requiring further information referring to the shorthand writer."

The case was then opened by the counsel for Major Anson. He explained that Major Anson had carried out a canvass of all the electors in the constituency, and the canvass was apparently a highly successful one; but the result of the poll was very different from what the canvass had led him to expect, it being as follows—

---

* Mr Justice Willes had been one of the four judges in Swinfen v Swinfen at the Court of Common Pleas in 1857.

Col. Dyott, 525; Major Anson 474. There was therefore a majority of 51 for Col. Dyott. This result the petitioner attributed to several causes. First of all, and primarily, he attributed it to bribery and intimidation by Col. Dyott himself; and thirdly to a wholesale and extensive system of corrupt treating of the electors for the purpose of influencing their votes, before, after and during the election.

Various witnesses were then produced to give evidence, most of it being concerned with " treating." It is fairly obvious that a good deal of drinking still took place at election time in Lichfield, the public houses mentioned most frequently by witnesses being the Bluebell, in Rotton Row, the Turk's Head in Sandford Street, the Robin Hood in Frog Lane and the Fountain in Beacon Street. No doubt there were others. The usual procedure was for a meeting to be held, addressed by the candidate or one of his committee members, following which a hat would be passed round to provide a " kitty " for drinks. On one such an occasion at the Turk's Head, a witness stated that he had seen Col. Dyott put four sovereigns in the hat. As it was unlikely that the gallant Colonel would drink that much liquor, the inference was that he was treating.

Old customs die hard, and to many voters an election was still an opportunity to make a bit on the side, as in the case of the following witness:

John Deakin—" I am a labourer, living in the Stafford Road, Lichfield. At the last election I voted for Major Anson. Some days before the election I met Mr John Valentine Hall, of Lincroft, near the Constitution Inn. He said ' You are just the person I want to see. Come and have a glass of ale.' I said, ' Thank you; I have no objection.' I went with him to the Constitution, where he asked me which way I intended to vote. I said I was not compelled to vote for either party. and I would vote for those who behaved the best to me (laughter). He paid for something to drink for me, and said that he had left some more for the next day . . . Some time before the election Mr Hall told me that he and Mr Graham* would see the doctors bill paid if I voted the way he

---

* Rev. John Graham, Rector of St Chad's.

wanted me to. It was £11.10 I owed Mr Welchman for attending me when I had the fever . . . I was disposed to vote for anyone that would pay me. It was my intention to get as much as I could, being a poor man."

Mr Dowdeswell (cross-examining) " You stand there and tell us so, and are not ashamed of it?"

Witness—" I am not ashamed at all."

The next to be called was Charles Deakin, father of the last witness. He too had been canvassed by Mr Hall, on behalf of Colonel Dyott. In the course of conversation witness had hinted that he would most likely vote for Major Anson. He also intimated that he had never been in a train; that he would much like to experience that mode of travel, and had several times considered the possibility of travelling either to Birmingham or to Tamworth to visit some of his relatives. Mr Hall thought that this was an excellent idea, and suggested that a visit to one of these salubrious spots should be made on the day of the election. In such a case, he hinted, he, Mr Hall, would meet the cost of a return ticket.

There was more along the same lines from other witnesses, but none of it seems to have impressed Mr Justice Willes very much, for in the end he confirmed Col. Dyott's election as M.P. for Lichfield and the Conservatives continued to hold the seat.

At the General Election of 1874, Col. Dyott was opposed by that stalwart Liberal, Charles Simpson.* At the age of 74 Mr Simpson was still Town Clerk, Coroner and Clerk of the Peace for Lichfield; now he was seeking pastures new. Since the last election the secret ballot had been introduced in 1872. How much this affected the result is difficult to say, but Dyott romped home with a majority of 141. But Charles Simpson was not disgraced; the Victorians admired pluck and a good fighter, and the city got together to provide him with a testimonial of their esteem. Many of his political opponents subscribed to it.

---

* Because he had supported all his life the institution of a secret ballot, he refused to canvass, or even to shake hands with voters, walking to his election meetings with his hands in his pockets.

The third and last petition against the election of an M.P. came six years later in 1880. In March of that year a General Election had returned Mr Gladstone as Prime Minister, but in spite of the Liberal swing Col. Dyott had managed to retain his seat by the narrow margin of sixteen votes. Sir John Swinburne, the Liberal candidate, petitioned against the result, and once again a judicial enquiry assembled at Lichfield Guildhall on Monday, 28th June. This time there were two judges, Justices Lush and Mainsty. Once again most of the evidence referred to " treating." Prominent among Col. Dyott's supporters were two of his fellow-officers of the Staffordshire Militia, Colonel Talbot and Adjutant Crauford. These two gentlemen spent their time touring the pubs in the days just before the election. " Any Militiamen here?" they would ask, and if there were Adjutant Crauford would buy them a drink and advise them to vote for Dyott. " Surely I can buy a drink for one of my own Militiamen " was his reply when accused of treating.

In the course of their perambulations the Colonel and his Adjutant (obviously following the military maxim that attack is the best defence), entered the Bald Buck Inn, on Greenhill, which was one of the Liberal Committee Rooms. Here, according to our witness, William Davis, Master Wheelwright, " the kitchen of the Bald Buck was full of men, but the beer came in too fast for them." One of the men asked Adjutant Crauford if he could not have some for the next night, and a half-sovereign was tendered and accepted. Edwin Smith, coal dealer, gave evidence that upon the first night they had about ten or eleven half-gallons of beer. The time was so short that they could not drink it all; what remained was poured into a jar and taken away.

There was a great deal more evidence along the same lines, and after a hearing which lasted four days the two judges found some of the accusations and they declared that the election of Col. Dyott was invalid.

The result was a Pyrric victory for Sir John Swinburne, the petitioner. At the ensuing bye-election Colonel Levett, the new Tory candidate, was returned with an increased majority. But as far as Richard Dyott was concerned, it was the end of his political career, after no less than 46 years. The " Lichfield Mercury," at that time a supporter of the Liberal cause had this to say:

" The quietude which succeeded the hurricane of Monday morning testified to the depth of feeling with which the unseating of Colonel Dyott was regarded, even by his enemies. A Parliamentary connection of fifteen years has been ruthlessly, though judicially, severed; but now that the desire of his opponents has accomplished, the separation was greater than had been contemplated, and they literally stood amazed at the success of their machinations. The leaders of the Liberal party had held aloof from the proceedings, and many had expressed their strong repugnance to a line of action fraught with such consequences to the peace and prosperity of the city. Sir John Swinburne, who did not claim the seat, had taken, they declared, the onus upon his own shoulders, and to him, therefore, must be awarded the credit for the victory. The decision of the judges had rested on two important infractions of the law; and although twenty and eight other charges had been disproved or abandoned, the penalty was inflicted in respect of an act the vital part of which, it is confidently asserted, will be clearly disproved. On the evidence before them, however, the judges declared that Colonel Dyott was not duly elected, and consequently the city, for the second time in three months, is in the heat of a political contest. It would ill-become the only public journal in the city to pass in silence over the varied phases of Colonel Dyott's long connection with Lichfield, and in bearing testimony to his devotion to his duties we confidently believe we express the feelings even of those who are diammetrically opposed to his political tenets. . . . The result of the petition has unseated Colonel Dyott whose Parliamentary connection thus ends in a sudden, and to him disheartening manner. This is particularly hard, as the gallant ex-member, throughout the enquiry, was exculpated from all blame, the seat being voided by the infractions already referred to. With Colonel Dyott's political opinions we have nothing to do, but we unhesitatingly record that the city has never been more faithfully served than during the years he has been in Parliament. Ever in the division lists, always alive to local interests, wonderfully anxious to serve his constituents, attentive to local celebrations, he has, in these respects at least, provoked the encomiums of his opponents and earned the gratitude of those whose political opinions he represents. And now the keen edge of the present situation is abated, it is hoped that Colonel Dyott—wonderfully hale as he is for a man who has passed the allotted three score years and ten—will not in the least withdraw himself from the city which has honoured him so greatly for the last fifteen years. His appearance here will be the more welcome, for in a non-political capacity he will not provoke that feeling of opposition which is inseparable from the position he has so lately occupied. And, moreover, a generous sympathy, not merely from his late supporters, but from his direst political opponents, should be the outcome of an event which has been received in Lichfield with such very mixed feelings."

Colonel Dyott followed the advice of the editor; he did not take any further part in politics, and at the next election in 1885 Sir John Swinburne captured the seat for the Liberals.

Colonel Dyott died in February 1891, and his funeral is still spoken of today, for it was the last occasion on which an old funeral tradition of the Dyott family was observed. It had been customary, ever since the days of the Commonwealth, for Dyotts to be buried at night, in the family vault at St Mary's Church. The origin of this custom is unknown, but it had been faithfully observed up to the time of the Colonel. Unfortunately two recent interments of members of the family had attracted the attention of many of that section of society which is drawn to such events by curiosity. It was presumably for this reason that the Vicar and Churchwardens of St Mary's issued the notice, a copy of which appears overleaf.

The night of 19th February was dark, for a dense fog hung over Lichfield as the funeral procession set out from Freeford Manor precisely at 9 o'clock. At the wish of Richard Dyott there were no flowers, no plumes on the hearse and no crape. A carriage conveying the High Sheriff of Staffordshire, Mr S. L. Seckham, led the procession with torch bearers on either side. Another carriage

THE FUNERAL OF THE LATE
COLONEL DYOTT,

OF FREEFORD HALL, IN

ST. MARY'S CHURCH, LICHFIELD,

On Thursday, February the 19th, 1891,

AT 10-0 P.M.

Those who may wish to attend the funeral are earnestly requested to remember the sacred solemnity of the place and the occasion.

Let these be perfect order and reverence in the Service, and **no standing on the Seats.**

At the conclusion of the Service there must be no pressure towards the Vault, **where there is nothing now visible;** but the congregation is requested at once quietly to disperse.

The last of an honoured Name has gone; let us lay his mortal part to rest with affectionate and reverential solemnity and order.

MELVILLE H. SCOTT, Vicar of S. Mary's.

THOMAS H HUNT, }
CHARLES TRIGG, } Churchwardens.

PRINTED BY A. C. LOMAX, THE "JOHNSON'S HEAD," LICHFIELD

followed carrying other dignitaries, and behind that walked the undertaker and the coffin maker, followed by eight underbearers carrying torches. The hearse came after, drawn by four horses and with four torchbearers on either side. Two more carriages carried the Colonel's agent and his butler and members of the family. As the procession passed through the park and out along the Tamworth Road it presented an eerie and solemn sight.

In the city, crowds began to gather as ten o'clock drew near. Many of them had been passing the time in the public houses, having come in from the surrounding villages. St Mary's Church was filled with a congregation of those who had come to pay their last respects, including members of the Magistracy, the Board of Guardians, the Military and the Constitutional Club, with all of which Colonel Dyott had been connected. The centre aisle was lined by a guard of honour of colour-sergeants from the Colonel's former unit, the 3rd Staffordshire Militia, now the 3rd Bn. The North Staffordshire Regt. The last persons to arrive were the Mayor and Corporation, preceded by the Sword and Maces draped in black.

The procession arrived outside the church just as the clock was striking ten, and it was at this point that the crowds caused what the press described as " unseemly bustling and noise." Inside the church the service proceeded in the simple fashion requested by the dead man; no music, no hymns, but just the reading of the Burial Service, during which the coffin was deposited in the vault.

So ended an ancient Lichfield tradition, and from then on members of the Dyott family were interred at Whittington Church without the nocturnal ceremony.

CHAPTER XI

Fin de Siècle

Compared with what had gone before, the last quarter of the 19th century passed almost without incident in Lichfield. There were no bank crashes, no notable criminal cases or lawsuits, no new and exciting developments such as railway building or waterworks schemes. Few new buildings were erected or old ones swept away, but among the latter was the Theatre Royal in Bore Street. In the words of a Lichfield writer who knew it, " Its demolition was almost an act of vandalism, for a discreet restoration would have secured a real theatre for a very lengthy period . . ." *

The last performances took place on the 12th and 13th of December, 1872, and in due course its place was taken by the St James's Hall on the same site. This was an assembly hall, used throughout the next forty years for meetings, lectures, occasional plays and County Balls. Here is how the Mercury reported one of these latter functions in 1880.

" Last night St James's Hall was once more the scene of a grand county gathering, the occasion being the annual County Ball. In spite of its Stafford rival it continues to assert its popularity, and if at times the numbers present fall short of former occasions, yet as a rule the proportions of the hall are taxed to their utmost by the representatives of the county families. This was the case last night, the attendance being upward of 200, a very fair average when contrasted with former gatherings. The ballroom presented the usual appearance, foliage and colour having been employed in a very artistic manner."

---

* " Lichfield," by Alfred Parker, Lomax, Lichfield, 1925.

The Lady Patroness of the evening was Lady Jane Levett; Stewards Sir Arthur Scott, Major Lane, Howard Paget Esq., Colonel Buller, Captain Manley, Coldstreams Guards, and M. Madan Esq.

Mr Gladman's band occupied the stage and performed waltzes by Waldteufel, Highland Schottiches, quadrilles and lancers by D'Albert and Offenbach. Mr and Mrs Trevor of the Swan Hotel were responsible, we are told, for the refreshments, " which were in every way admirable."

County Balls at St James's Hall lasted until 1907. In the following year the march of technology turned the hall into a cinema (still remembered by many as " The Palladium "). From then on the County Ball moved to the George Hotel, where a large marquee in the inn yard accommodated the dancers. Like so many other institutions, Lichfield's County Ball ended in the upheaval of the 1914 war.

Another social occasion which came to an end in the last years of Victoria's reign was Lichfield's Race Week. For nearly two centuries the Race Weeks had been two of the big social events of the year, and though they had decreased in importance throughout the 19th century as other racecourses were opened up, they were still very popular. But in 1877 the War Office began to build a new barracks on Whittington Heath. In due course it became the depot of the North Staffordshire and South Staffordshire Regiments. But the War Office were not happy to find a racecourse at the barrack gates, and the area of the common on which it was situated was requisitioned for training purposes. The last races were held in 1895, and the grandstand became a Soldiers' Home and canteen.

To build the barracks large numbers of labourers were brought in from outside, mainly from Ireland. They and their families were housed in old disused railway carriages which were raised on brick piers along both sides of the road which now runs past the Regimental Museum. It being the age of puns, this thoroughfare was known as the High Street. Bricks for building the barracks were made at Aldridge and brought by canal to Huddlesford, from where a two-foot gauge railway carried them over the common to the building site.

Another event in 1877 was the establishment of a Lichfield weekly newspaper. For some forty years the city had been without a permanent weekly journal; several attempts to start one had failed after a short time, but this time success was to crown the efforts of the promoters. The first issue of the new paper appeared on Friday, 28th September, 1877, and the leading article ran as follows:

" In presenting the first number of the Lichfield Mercury to the public of Lichfield and the neighbourhood, we are aware that its name will recall the existence of a former Lichfield newspaper of a similar title. The old Lichfield Mercury, which was established during the stirring times of the first Napoleon, was in its day no ordinary venture, for it presented a sheet of twenty columns, and it numbers, particularly at the period of its establishment, were brimful of interest. It seems strange that for so many years journalistic enterprise, so far as a locally published paper is concerned, has been practically dead, but it remains to be seen whether the increasing population and the prospective important additions to our city and neighbourhood do not offer a field for the successful exercise of diligence in the direction we have indicated. There can be little doubt that a properly conducted weekly newspaper, professing independent opinions in Imperial and local politics, the organ of no sect or party, reporting fully and fairly all events of local interest and edited with discretion, will appeal—and that successfully—to a population embracing nearly twenty thousand people . . . "

The article finished with a quotation from Addison, " It is not in mortals to command success, but we'll do more—we'll deserve it."

No one would deny that today, after 100 years, the Lichfield Mercury has lived up to the words of its first Editor.

Items of local news in this first edition included a report of the theft of a lady's gown, value £4 10s, from the " Prince of Wales " Inn; an attempted suicide by strangling by an army recruit who had been incarcerated in the cells under the Guildhall by the Police for being drunk and disorderly; a warning that counterfeit money (mainly shillings) was circulating in the city; a report of a performance of " The Octaroon " and " Little Emily " at St James's Hall with Mr Eldred getting a special mention for his portrayal of Micawber, and a report that the officers of the 24th (Lichfield) Staffordshire Volunteer Corps had decided to approach the public for subscriptions to purchase prizes for their shooting competitions, which were to be held at Rugeley Ranges in October. There was also a list of subscribers to an appeal fund for defraying the cost of restoring the West Front of the Cathedral, which was just getting under way. A sum of £20,000 was being asked for. There had also been collections at the Cathedral and in all the Churches for the Indian Famine Relief Fund, which had been "'liberally supported."

Among the advertisements in the classified columns was one from someone calling herself " Side Saddle," Birmingham, who wished to ride ladies horses for the hunting field, and another from Mr Thos. Oakes, Grocer, Chasetown, who had " Freehold building land for sale, pleasantly situated," at eightpence per square yard.

The 24th (Lichfield) Staffordshire Volunteers just referred to were part of the Volunteer Movement (The " Home Guard " of that period) which had come into being in 1859 when there was a threat of war with France. All over the country committees were set up to organise a local corps and raise money for their equipment and training. At Lichfield the first meeting was held on 30th November, 1859, at which the 24th was formed. Volunteer Rifle Corps, being autonomous and self-financing to a high degree, made their own decisions on the colour and design of their uniforms (which were often highly original) and such things as their titles. The Rugeley Corps, for example, referred to themselves as the Rugeley Rangers. The Volunteers were very much a citizens' army and a natural target for jokes in Punch, just as the Home Guard has been in more recent times. It has never been the habit of the British people, on the surface, to take amateur soldiers too seriously.

In 1883, following the re-organisation of the Regular Army on County Regiment lines, the volunteer forces were similarly treated and the 24th (Lichfield) Staffordshire Volunteers became the Lichfield Company of the 2nd Volunteer Battalion, North Staffordshire Regt. and in due course part of the Territorial Army, trained and organised on the same lines as the Regular Army. Even so, when the Lichfield Company wanted their own drill-hall, they had to build it themselves in Frog Lane, raising the money by public subscription.

In passing, it is worth mentioning to what extent this aspect of public life prevailed in Victorian times. Today we are so used to the state financing almost every aspect of our lives that it is hard to believe that so much depended on private effort. It applied not only to drill-halls, but also to industrial schools (where the rehabilitation of young offenders was undertaken), to many of the ordinary elementary schools, to hospitals and clinics. Even fire engines came into this category; the first motor fire engine to be used by the Lichfield Fire Brigade was the gift of Mr Worthington of Maple Hayes.

Throughout the whole of the 19th century one of the high spots of each year, vying in popularity with race weeks and elections, was the Yeomanry Week, when the county yeomanry regiment, The Queen's Own Royal Staffordshire Yeomanry, gathered in Lichfield for training.

The Q.O.R.W. has a long history, having been founded in 1794. It was sometimes referred to as Volunteer Cavalry, and like the Volunteer Rifles, it was recruited from civilians who trained in their spare time. Unlike the Riflemen, however, the Yeomanry drew its members from the upper strata of society; officers came from the county aristocracy and in the words of a newspaper of the 1880s, " Gentlemen of position are content to join the Regiment as troopers, and if this is not a new feature, it is one which bespeaks the esteem in which the regiment is held." Most of the officers had been through the ranks in this way.

The Yeomanry Week, held in June, was looked forward to by most of the people in Lichfield. Here is how the Lichfield Mercury described it in 1882.

" Lichfield will be en fête next week on the annual occasion
of the training of this regiment. The regiment ranks among the
highest of its class, being generally regarded as the most efficient
in the country, and Staffordshire is naturally very proud of the
fame which it has acquired. The annual assembly of the regiment
at Lichfield is always anticipated with great interest, and if the
weather proves fine, Yeomanry week is invariably one of the most
pleasant and enjoyable occasions of the year. The city usually
assumes its brightest appearance, tradesmen and others vie in their
efforts to make an attractive display, and the streets become
unwontedly animated and gay."

The week began on Saturday, when the various troops rode
into the city from all over the county. As well as the Lichfield
Troop there were the Stafford Troop, Newcastle Troop, Himley
Troop, Wolverhampton Troop, Walsall Troop and the Leek,
Cheadle and Uttoxeter Troops. They arrived from midday
onwards and paraded in the Market Place from where they
dispersed to their billets in the various hostelries around the city.
The officers' mess was at the Swan.

On Sunday morning they paraded, dismounted, on Levett's
Field, by the railway station, and led by their band marched to the
Cathedral for a service. The Infantry Volunteers usually
accompanied them, and all Lichfield turned out to watch. During
the week they paraded daily at nine o'clock on Levett's Field and
marched, 530 strong, to Whittington Heath for drill. At six every
evening they met for further drill at the Cricket Ground on the
Birmingham Road. One wonders what the groundsman thought
about having 500 horses walking over his pitch in the middle of
the season, especially as at that time Lichfield was the home ground
of the county team. In the previous decade there had been attempts
to stage a Lichfield Cricket Festival, during which Lichfield Cricket
Club had taken on All-England sides,* but it did not catch on.

---

* It should be added that on these occasions, while the All England teams
consisted of the conventional eleven men, Lichfield fielded twenty-two
men. They still lost.

A lot went on during the evenings of Yeomanry week. Each troop had its troop dinner, there were smoking concerts and at the Theatre or later St James's Hall, there was special entertainment for the week.

In the year 1884 this was provided by Mr D'Oyly Carte's No. 2 Touring Company of " Princess Ida," the latest of Messers Gilbert and Sullivan's Savoy Operas. On the Thursday evening, 15th June, there was a large contingent of Yeomanry in the audience, and they were feeling more than usually exuberant. Probably the excellent and renowned ale of the Lichfield Brewery Company had something to do with it. At any rate, several times during the evening the performance was stopped by noisy interruptions from the Yeomen, and during the interval several of them mounted the stage and raised one of the trapdoors, by means of which it was possible to get access to the ladies' dressing room. Pandemonium ensued, and it was some time before order was restored.

These interruptions were not appreciated by the rest of the audience, and after the show there were angry arguments outside the theatre in Bore Street. Fighting broke out, a crowd soon gathered, and on the basis of Is-this-a-private-battle-or-can-anyone-join-in? before long a proper shindy had broken out. It spread to little groups outside the various hostelries at which Yeomen were billeted. At this time Lichfield's Police Force consisted of only six men, and they decided, very properly, to keep out of the way. But when news of the fracas reached the Officers' Mess at the Swan, Colonel Bromley-Davenport, the Commanding Officer, and Captain Graves, his adjutant, sallied forth to put a stop to this undignified brawling. Outside the Robin Hood in St John St. (now the City Gates), poor Colonel Bromley-Davenport had a heart attack and fell dead. As the news spread around order was restored and the city became quiet. The rest of the week was carried out in a very restrained manner, overshadowed by the tragedy of Thursday night.

Like the Volunteers, Yeomanry were only engaged for the home defence of their country, and for giving assistance to the Civil Power (which frequently happened in the early years of Queen Victoria's reign; the Staffordshire Yeomanry were called out no less than sixty times in their history). With the growth of police forces this latter use became unnecessary, and by the eighties and nineties there were those who looked upon the Yeomanry as something of a dilettante army which young men joined more for social reasons than for anything else. This is reflected in the speeches of their officers at troop dinners, when their men were exhorted to " mean business."

A chance to do this came in the last year of the Queen's reign, when, with the increased need for troops to fight in South Africa, where the war was not going at all well for the British, the Imperial Yeomanry was formed with volunteers from the various county regiments. Those from Staffordshire formed the 6th Company, 4th Battalion Imperial Yeomanry, and one cold and dark night in January 1900 they entrained at Lichfield City Station for the war. From then on it was very much a matter of business. The days of roses and wine were past, and in 1914 and 1939 the whole regiment of the Staffordshire Yeomanry was embodied as soon as war broke out.

Queen Victoria died on the 22nd of January, 1901. She had just lived long enough to see the beginning of the twentieth century, and had reigned for sixty-four years. In that time Lichfield, in common with the rest of the country had moved out of an age in which little had changed from the time of the Romans to one in which houses were lit by electric light (the first house in Lichfield had it in 1894), messages could be sent to any part of the globe by telegraph, while Marconi had already sent experimental signals by wireless, through the aether. Trains had supplanted horses, and now the internal combustion engine had come to take the place of steam engines. Peoples' attitudes to each other had changed, too; there were fewer deaths from disease or poverty; everyone had a chance of some education and all males could vote in elections. Housing had improved (Lichfield built its first municipal houses in St John St. in the 1890s; one of the first municipal authorities to do so). But some things remained unchanged; the old traditions of the Bower, the Sheriff's Ride and the Manorial Courts; but above all the feeling of affection common to all true Lichfield citizens for the " Ancient and Loyal City " to which they belong.

THE END

Index